Indian Managers and Organizations

T0300081

Culture is critical to individuals and organizations. This book takes a close look into the way Indian managers work, their inner struggles, and forces that shape their behavior. It presents an original framework developed by the author – the Existential Universe Mapper (EUM), a pluralistic and non-reductionist model that uses a new psychometric instrument to map individual and organization identity. The model restrains from placing any phenomenon into frozen categories and enables an understanding of their interplay. The volume points to India's ambivalent relationship with modernity and the consequent difficulty of Indian managers in embracing the imperatives of the corporate world that are largely based on Anglo-Saxon frames.

With analyses based on data from more than 100 organizations and 4,500 managers, the book argues that the gap between the Indian cultural perspective and the prevalent ways of the corporate world is both a boon and a burden. An integration of the two perspectives could help achieve phenomenal results and this may well be the way forward in the global context.

This book will be of interest to those in business management, human resource management, leadership studies, corporate governance, industries, education, social sector, governance, psychology and sociology. It will be particularly relevant for scholars, educators, consultants, practitioners of management and corporate leaders. Professionals who employ psychometric tools, recruitment firms, coaches and consultants involved with assessment centers, career planning, counseling and mentoring will find it extremely useful.

Ashok Malhotra is an independent management consultant based in Bengaluru, India, with nearly five decades of experience of working with individuals, groups and organizations in the areas of personal growth and organization development. He is one of the founders of the Sumedhas Academy for Human Context and has published books, several articles in professional journals, and presented papers in many national and international conferences. His earlier book *Child Man: The Selfless Narcissist* was published in 2010 and has received acclaim.

This reflective and sophisticated work shows how Indian managers negotiate two different perspectives: their civilizational predispositions and their Indianness, and the imperatives of their corporate role that have their roots in modern Western civilization. With its solid empirical foundations, brilliant insights and wide-ranging scholarship, this book is an invaluable guide not only for students and practitioners of management but for all those who are interested in the interplay, often uneasy, between the workings of traditional cultures and a West-centric modernity.

    – Sudhir Kakar, psychoanalyst, novelist and scholar

This is an important and deeply perceptive book that uses data collected over the years to mark the evolution of, not just the Indian manager, but also of the educated, urban Indian over the last few decades. This book will become a standard work on the subject.

    – Vir Sanghvi, print and TV journalist and author

A much-needed book as most writings about India are filtered through Western lens. This book is a refreshing change as it delves deep into the Indian identity of the present. A must-read for contemporary Indians to find their freedom from the mortgages of the past, and discover their own uniqueness.

    – Indira J. Parikh, President, Antardisha and Professor and former Dean, Indian Institute of Management-Ahmedabad

The book fascinates. It offers a kind of symphony for life and work for the Indian managers amidst the noise within. Ashok is incisive. He is tender as well as he unravels the struggles with the dualities of

two dominant intrinsic identities – the Indian and the Western – an Indian manager lives and works with.
– **Shomu Acharya,** CEO, eTrans Solutions, India

This book is an insightful analysis that would be of great value to business leaders and managers who are interested to understand the complexity of Indian work life and family life.
– **Ajeet Mathur,** Professor, Indian Institute of Management-Ahmedabad

A must-read for those who believe traditionalism impedes, even the twenty-first century Indian manager from embracing modern corporatism. The author provides deep insights into the reason as also the potential and ideas to co-hold these disparate yet powerful belief systems.
– **L. Lakshman,** Chairman Emeritus, RANE Group, India

Ashok Malhotra, through this book answers the question *"Is there a way of looking at the Indian psyche that is insightful, honest and dignifying?"* By adopting frames of reference that do not fit us, we do great disservice to ourselves and hold our propensities in doubt or shame. Ashok offers every Indian a framework backed by deep research that will provide a foundation for pride tempered by critical self-appraisal.
– **Raghu Anathanarayanan,** Director and Chief Consultant, FLAME TAO Knoware, India

Indian Managers and Organizations

Boons and Burdens

Ashok Malhotra

LONDON AND NEW YORK

First published 2019
by Routledge

2 Park Square, Milton Park, Abingdon, Oxfordshire OX14 4RN
52 Vanderbilt Avenue, New York, NY 10017

Routledge is an imprint of the Taylor & Francis Group, an informa business

First issued in paperback 2019

Copyright © 2019 Ashok Malhotra

The right of Ashok Malhotra to be identified as author of this
work has been asserted by him in accordance with sections 77
and 78 of the Copyright, Designs and Patents Act 1988.

All rights reserved. No part of this book may be reprinted
or reproduced or utilised in any form or by any electronic,
mechanical, or other means, now known or hereafter invented,
including photocopying and recording, or in any information
storage or retrieval system, without permission in writing from
the publishers.

Notice:
Product or corporate names may be trademarks or registered trademarks,
and are used only for identification and explanation without intent to infringe.

British Library Cataloguing-in-Publication Data
A catalogue record for this book is available from the British Library

Library of Congress Cataloging-in-Publication Data
A catalog record has been requested for this book

ISBN: 978-0-8153-5098-9 (hbk)
ISBN: 978-0-367-47935-0 (pbk)

Typeset in Sabon
by Apex CoVantage, LLC

For my grandson, Isaac, with a wish that he will co-hold his Indian heritage with European roots and upbringing

Contents

Illustrations

4.17	Comparison of desired shifts between EUM-I and EUM-O	81
7.1	Preservation versus transformation	140
7.2	Orientation of Indian managers in the first polarity	141
7.3	Meritocracy versus humanism	146
7.4	Orientation of Indian managers in the second polarity	147
7.5	Control versus empowerment	152
7.6	Orientation of Indian managers in the third polarity	152
7.7	Comparison of objective rationality versus subjective sensing	158
7.8	Orientation of Indian managers in the fourth polarity	158
7.9	Leadership orientation of Indian managers	160
8.1	Comparing the Homo economicus with the Homo reciprocans	169
8.2	Comparing the Rational Ingenieur with the Bricoleur	175
8.3	Comparing the agonic and the hedonic modes of centripetal collectives	181
8.4	Leadership implications of the two perspectives	187
9.1	Shifts needed at the individual level	197
9.2	Shifts needed at the organizational level	209

Appendices

Acknowledgments

This book has only my name as the author, but it is, in fact, a collective endeavor of the entire EUM group – Gagandeep Singh, Sarbari Gomes, K.S. Narendran, Abhay Phadnis, Snigdha Nautiyal and me. Hence, except in Chapter 2, which deals with the evolution of EUM, I have used the plural *we* because many of the insights emerged in our collective deliberations.

While every member of the EUM group has contributed significantly, a special mention needs to be made of Gagandeep Singh. The Hema–Ravi case, which provides the running thread through the book, has been written by him. He has also written and significantly modified many other parts particularly in Chapter 8.

There are also several other people who have been my co-travelers in the EUM Journey. To begin with there were my colleagues at the erstwhile Mafoi Management Consultants, including K.P. Rajan, Latha Rajan, K.S. Narendran, Abhay Phadnis, Mustafa Moochala, Vijay Nair and C.S. Mahesh.

Raghu Ananthanarayanan has been a significant source of support. Right from its initial days, Raghu not merely helped me to work on the framework but also contributed significantly to its deployment.

The chapter on Indianness draws heavily from an event on this theme organized by Sumedhas Academy for Human Context.

I am grateful to Dr. Sudhir Kakar, Shri Vir Sanghvi, Dr. Indira J. Parikh, Dr. Ajeet Mathur, Shri Raghu Ananthnarayanan, Shri L. Lakshman, Shri S.K. Acharya, Shri S.V. Nathan, Shri Pratap G and Shri Mustafa Moochala for their valuable inputs on the manuscript.

This book would not have materialized but for the 5,000 managers and leaders across Indian and global firms that have subscribed to the profiling, coaching and dialogic interventions.

Over a period of two decades, a set of 100-plus organizations have invited us to work with them on aspects of culture change, leadership building and coaching, trusting the underlying framework and its effectiveness.

I would like to acknowledge more than 100-plus professionals, coaches and leaders who have been certified to work with the EUM instruments and have partnered our research.

Abbreviations

EUM	Existential Universe Mapper
EUM-I	Existential Universe Mapper – Individual
EUM-O	Existential Universe Mapper – Organizational
MOO	Most Other Organizations
OC	Organization Current
OI	Organization Ideal
OP	Other People
SC	Self Current
SI	Self Ideal
UBP	Universe of Belonging & Protection
UDS	Universe of Duality & Simultaneity
UMI	Universe of Meaningfulness & Intimacy
UPA	Universe of Purpose & Achievement
URB	Universe of Roles & Boundaries
USD	Universe of Strength & Desire
WIIFM	What's in it for me?

Chapter 1

Introduction

Indianness is sometimes glorified and sometimes condemned but rarely understood. Mostly, the discourse around it remains either focused on past greatness or on regressive social practices like the caste system. Hence, one often comes across Indians who love their country but have scant respect for their fellow countrymen and -women. While they take considerable pride in our glorious past, great heritage, ancient wisdom, spiritual values, sophisticated philosophy and so on, this pride is rarely reflected in what they think about the kind of people that we are.

A simple Google search on "Indian character" will throw up many more negatives than positives. Even in casual conversations, there are frequent references to Indian hypocrisy, duplicity, double standards, lack of civic sense, clannish/parochial mind-set, crab mentality, frog-in-the-well attitude, inability to confront directly, cowardice and passive aggression, among others. The list is endless.

While these negative associations exist, there is also the reality that today many large global organizations (e.g., Microsoft, Google, Adobe, Pepsi, etc.) are headed by people of Indian origin. It is not possible to say whether Indianness has played any part in the success of these individuals, or is it simply a matter of coincidence that they happen to be of Indian origin? In fact, the more commonly held sentiment is that it is the meritocratic American culture that has enabled these people to transcend the limitations of their Indian context. However, slowly but surely, a mystique has started to get built around Indian managers.

Several large multinationals have started specifically looking for people of Indian origin for their leadership positions. We were recently told by a senior human resources (HR) professional that the unstated norm is to have at least 20% of candidates of Indian origin in any short list for a senior position.

Thus, it would seem that with all its negative associations, Indianness could also be a resource and, in some inexplicable manner, a contributing factor in leadership and managerial effectiveness.

Whether Indianness is a liability or an asset is a question which would require us to dig deeper into the essence of Indianness rather than looking at it merely as history, traditions and/or personality traits of people living in the geopolitical entity called India. In this book, we have attempted to engage with Indianness as a perspective – as a way of life and as a set of beliefs and assumptions about the human condition. In that sense, it would be fair to say that this perspective is not exclusive to people of India only. In other words, Indians do not have a monopoly over Indianness. The only thing one can say is that this perspective can be discerned more easily amongst people of the Indian subcontinent.

The central questions that this book addresses are, How does this perspective align with the imperatives of the times that we live in? Is it merely a relic of the past, or does it hold something of value in the present context? To begin with, it may be helpful to explore how India has engaged with the pulls and pushes of the modern times.

India and modernity

India's ambivalent relationship with modernity (i.e., the times that we live in) is visible in virtually all spheres of present-day life. On one hand, modernity is seen as a gateway to techno-economic progress, social justice and individual liberty, but on the other, it is also seen as a destabilizer that uproots individuals not merely from their heritage but, in a sense, from their own emotions and psychological predispositions. Not surprisingly, the ideal state, which many Indians aspire for, is one where the privileges of modernity can be integrated with the traditional Indian ways.

Many a politician, filmmaker, advertiser and so on have found tremendous success through promising this idyllic scenario. Take, for example, the case of Rajshri Productions[1] – most of its blockbusters (*Dulhan wahi jo piya man bhaye*, *Hum aapke hain kaun* and *Hum saath saath hein*, among others) are family sagas of rich business families who enjoy all the modern-day creature comforts and are reasonably progressive in their outlook yet also show strong adherence to traditional Indian values like familial ties, respect for elders, religiosity and so on. The same formula can be witnessed in countless television serials in all Indian languages, which enjoy high viewership and popularity. It would be reasonable to assume that beneath the popularity of these films and serials lies a deeper search to integrate modernity with tradition. In this idyllic scenario, the inherent conflict and tension is either wished away or resolved through vilification of modernity.

The situation gets a lot more complex when we move out of the social/familial realm and enter the world of work organizations and corporate offices. Since the basic foundation of these systems rests on Anglo-Saxon frames of management, leadership and nature of systems, it is neither possible to deny the tension nor to resolve it through vilification of modernity. Consequently, often the individual tries to resolve the tension and resultant ambivalence, by repressing his or her Indianness (civilizational predispositions) and/ or treating it as a liability to be overcome. In other words, the individual begins to believe that while his/her Indianness has a legitimate space in familial/social systems, his or her engagements with task systems should be governed by notions of "professionalism" that are largely Anglo-Saxon in nature.

Civilizational predispositions are not a piece of clothing, which can be changed or discarded at will. These have come to us over generations both through the genetic codings and the processes of socialization and acculturation.

Simultaneously, these are not tight prisons, which leave no room for individual freedom and volition. Each one of us has considerable freedom to choose what we wish to do with our civilizational heritage, but this choice can only be exercised meaningfully by first understanding and acknowledging it.

When it is repressed, or denied, it does not go away but only becomes invisible to us and thus casts its shadows in ways, which we remain largely unaware of. Thus, many Indian managers overtly subscribe to the norms and practices prescribed by these systems, but their intrinsic psychic disposition keeps pulling them in another direction.

For example, at the rational level, they may accept that authority relationships should be configured on "adult-to-adult" basis, but in their emotive maps, the relationship remains configured on a "parent–child" frame.

When this schism (between the cognitive and the emotive) is seen through frameworks that are reductionist and based on Aristotelean binaries[2] of "either–or", all we can see is a host of inconsistencies and contradictions. Thus, if faith and reason are seen as mutually exclusive categories, then it becomes difficult to understand as to how a person with scientific temperament can also consult an astrologer to find an auspicious date for starting a new venture.

In order to understand how these seemingly contradictory positions are negotiated in the Indian mind, we require a framework that is holistic, which does not place phenomena into frozen categories, and which enables an understanding of the interplay between different variables rather than studying them in isolation.

As we shall see in the next chapter, these have been the most important considerations in the evolution of the EUM Framework, which has been used for our empirical data. Consequently, this book is as much about the *lens* as it is about the *phenomenon*, which is being observed through the lens.

Lens and phenomenon

All frameworks/lenses rest on some basic assumptions and consequently determine what are the relevant facts to be taken into account and how they are to be interpreted. For example, a framework, which is based on the belief that human beings essentially operate from the principle of "rational self-interest", will primarily focus on the tangible costs and benefits of a transaction and ignore the dynamics of feelings and relationships. Similarly, phenomena such as love and compassion have a very different meaning from an evolutionary perspective as compared to a religious/spiritual perspective. From an evolutionary point of view, they can be treated as "reciprocal arrangements" that have helped human beings to survive and evolve. However, from a religious/spiritual perspective they are more likely to be treated as "virtues" that are required for human salvation and/or dictates from the Almighty.

Most frameworks (though by no means all) tend to use mutually exclusive categories. This is particularly applicable to frameworks, which are binary in nature (e.g., introversion–extroversion, dominance–submission, masculine–feminine, etc.).

While the placement of people/phenomenon in clear categories/types helps in a broad and general appreciation/understanding, it also undermines their uniqueness and finer nuances. We believe this is particularly so when the framework is incongruent with the salient features of the culture in which the phenomenon is taking place. Thus, deference towards age/seniority may be regarded as a sign of "dependency" in a framework where the basic assumption is that each individual is an autonomous being and generational conflict is seen as an inevitable component of the maturation process. However, the same behavior will have a very different meaning in another framework, which looks at the individual as a relational being and looks at the maturation process in terms of extending the traditional values rather than rupturing them. In such a scenario, equating deference with dependency can be misleading.

The EUM lens

The emphasis in the EUM framework is on PLURALITY and INTERPLAY. Its central premise is that all human beings are remarkably similar and yet unique. Each one of us is born with unique genetic codings in a unique family/community. In the process of growing up we receive our own specific messages and have our unique life experience to which we give our unique meanings and make our individual choices. All this and more makes us the unique person that each one of us becomes. Yet behind this uniqueness, all human beings are remarkably similar. We are all governed by laws of nature and by biological/psychic imperatives of being human. We all seek fulfillment of our physical needs, safety of belonging, personal freedom, control over our destiny, warmth and intimacy, meaningful purpose for our lives and so on. Needless to say, the configuration of these different elements varies from person to person, but the essential elements remain the same.

Thus, for some of us personal freedom may be more important whereas others may place greater emphasis on the need to belong. Similarly, the way we engage with these elements may differ. Some people may deal with their need for safety by running away from danger whereas others may become aggressive and prefer to take it head-on. Irrespective of whether one responds to danger through "flight" or "fight" and in some rare cases through "equanimity" we all have to come to terms with and learn to live with our need for safety.

In this sense, every human being can be regarded as a unique but dynamic configuration of same basic elements. Consequently, it is futile to put people into different categories. Instead it would be more meaningful to understand the nature of their unique configurations and the interplay between the different aspects of themselves.

In the EUM framework, these different aspects are seen in terms of six Universes that reside within each person. Each Universe is seen as a composite set of values, beliefs, needs, behaviors and so on. The detailed description of these Universes is provided in Chapter 3. As we will see later, what the EUM lens focuses on is the following:

a   The multiplicity which resides within each person
b   The interplay of these multiple parts and the resultant configuration
c   The dynamics of relatedness between the Self and the situation

Our approach

As mentioned earlier, all human beings are alike and unique. Between the two extremes of absolute uniqueness and complete commonality lies a huge middle ground. This middle ground is formed by the "collective context" that we share with other human beings to varying degrees. Thus, with people who belong to the same socioeconomic ethnic group, we may share much in terms of our basic socialization and acculturation. Similarly, with people who belong to the same professional group as us, we may share several beliefs and perspectives. Needless to say, these commonalities are not linear in nature. It is not unusual to experience great affinity with someone who may have very little in common with us.

In case of Indian managers, the two main determinants of this common ground are (a) civilizational predispositions and (b) corporate imperatives.

Civilizational predispositions

Like human beings, civilizations also differ from each other. While every civilization needs to deal with the same basic issues of human existence, there is considerable variance in the ways of their engagement. These variances arise from their unique life conditions including geopolitical history, culture, technology of living, social structures, religious practices and host of such factors. Over time, its basic way of living gets codified in the form of values, beliefs and predispositions that are passed on from generation to generation both through genetic codings and processes of socialization and acculturation. Needless to say, each individual person will have unique genetic codings as also unique experiences of socialization and acculturation. The civilizational context merely provides the broad container in which these individual experiences are held.

Corporate imperatives

Like all social arrangements, the world of corporates also has its unique imperatives and therefore fosters certain beliefs, values and behaviors that are most conducive for its needs. While each organization has its own unique culture, history, requirements, leadership/managerial orientations, they are held within a broad container, which may be called "the corporate way". Thus, themes like meritocracy, achievement orientation, teamwork, growth and continuous improvement, among others, are likely to be assumed as "self-evident" virtues in most organizations.

Therefore, characteristics, which are seen as helpful in this endeavor (e.g., ambition, assertiveness, effective interface management etc.), are likely to be valued by people who are part of the corporate world.

These two common grounds, that is, the "civilizational predispositions" and the "corporate way" have an interesting relationship with each other. The corporate way has largely evolved in the context of what may broadly be termed as Western civilizations. Consequently, it is likely to align well with the civilizational identity of people in those societies. However, in case of other societies (like India) the situation is a lot more complex. Several aspects of the two may align well with each other, but there may also be dissonance and areas of tension. It is important to recognize both the resonances and dissonances between the two so that these tensions can be meaningfully engaged with. In absence of such an understanding, the civilizational identity is likely to be repressed/suppressed leading to a large gap between espoused values/beliefs and actual behavior.

The book aims to look at the interplay between these two dimensions through the EUM lens. Given its emphasis on plurality and interplay, EUM provides a lens through which both these strands can be discerned and the convergence/divergence between them be explored.

Our experience, findings from the EUM data (from more than 100 Indian organizations covering more than 4,500 managers) and insights from other scholars suggest that the civilizational identity of Indian managers has an uneasy relationship with the imperatives of their role as managers. Importantly, these are not just differences in attitude and behavior but in much more basic nature as well. The differences in attitude and behavior are only manifestation of differences in underlying beliefs and assumptions about human existence. For example, the emphasis on the individual as a relational being rather than an autonomous being does not sit well with the principle of 'Homo economicus' on which the modern corporate world operates. Similarly, the preference for "context sensitivity" in the Indian mind is often at variance with a need for uniformity and universal applicability.

Not surprisingly, we find that managers in our sample are trying to engage with two seemingly opposite perspectives. This ambivalence is both a problem and an opportunity. On one hand, it creates stress and results in many compromises and dysfunctionalities, but on the other hand, it opens many creative possibilities. In fact, we have found that the effectiveness of Indian managers depends a great deal on how well they manage this tension. Furthermore, the balancing and/or co-holding of these divergent perspectives may be of considerable significance, beyond the Indian corporate world.

Limitation of our findings

Since a large part of our database is about Indian managers, we do not have sufficient comparative data about

a   managers of other nationalities and
b   people from other spheres of life (social activists, homemakers, government employees, students, farmers, artisans, etc.).

Thus, our findings have to be taken primarily for this group of people. To what extent they are also applicable to Indians, in general, and to people in the corporate world irrespective of their national identities is a matter of conjecture. Based on our own subjective experiences as also insights from other scholars we have tried to offer insights/hypotheses, but their empirical validity is necessarily limited.

Introducing the structure of the book

Since the focus of this book is on both the lens and the phenomenon, a degree of oscillation between the two is inevitable. In order to understand/appreciate our findings, the reader needs to acquire a degree of familiarity with the EUM framework. Consequently, the first two chapters are devoted to the EUM framework before we start looking at the data and explore their implications. The broad structure is as follows.

Chapter 2: evolution of EUM framework: a personal journey

This chapter links the author's personal journey, his own philosophical stances, his experiments, his thoughts and his writings that led to the creation of the EUM framework. It begins with a critique of binaries that underlie cognitive frameworks and leads on to his discovery of Clare Graves's work in his search of holistic frameworks. In this chapter, the author acknowledges Graves's work while also stating how the EUM framework is different from it in terms of possibilities and interpretation. The chapter hints at other influential writings, such as the works of Aurobindo and Chakras theory, that have a strong resonance with the EUM framework.

Chapter 3: EUM framework and tools

This chapter introduces the reader to the EUM framework as well as the two instruments – EUM-I and EUM-O – that have been applied and researched over the last many years. The chapter begins by articulating seven key axioms – termed as ideational foundations – that are fundamental to the definition of the framework, as well as differentiating it from other frames including Graves's Theory of Open Systems of Values. The chapter stresses on key constructs and language that are critical to understanding the EUM framework, including the term *Universe*. It endorses the notion of the term interplay of Universes as the key interpretative tool. The chapter also invites the reader to browse through Appendices 3.1 to 3.4, which explain the Universes in great detail, as well as familiarize her with the two tools.

Chapter 4: findings from EUM data

In this chapter, we present our understanding and analysis of the data collected from the two tools of EUM-I and EUM-O from more than 100 organizations and over 4,500 individuals. This chapter begins with part 1, which offers an analysis of EUM-I data and six themes that summarize the Indian manager's pulls and role taking. Part 2 offers an analysis of EUM-O data and its six themes. Part 3 takes both these data sets together, looks at complementarities and contradictions and culminates into a summary of the profile of the Indian manager. This chapter is replete with data tables and data analysis, offering themes and understandings as working hypotheses.

Chapter 5: an uneasy relationship

In this chapter, we use an illustrative case of two individuals – Hema and Ravi as archetypal identities that represent the inner battlefield of the Indian manager. On one hand, Ravi represents the left spiral of the EUM framework – emphasizing on tradition, whole systems, and collectives that get internalized within the Indian manager with all the virtues and blind spots. On the other hand, Hema represents the right side of the EUM spiral, symbolizing the world of modern market capitalism, its demands, its seductions and its oppressions. We believe that this is becoming more of an either–or as opposed to really integrating two powerful forces – and that mere balancing act is of little consequence.

The chapter offers an understanding of the three forces that play up – that of the agent, the structure and the communion as we look at the interplay of Hema and Ravi. The chapter begins a journey that continues in the subsequent chapters, laying down the principle of '*Jugaad*' and how it is more of a coping mechanism rather than an expression of Indian ingenuity.

Chapter 6: Indianness: the civilizational predispositions

This chapter is pivotal to the entire book, as it postulates the civilizational codings for the Indian manager – offering a series of perspectives on key fronts of sociopsychological themes of identity (Who am I?), context sensitivity, preoccupation with hierarchy, patriarchy and gender, and faith. On each of these fronts, the chapter offers insights and an understanding of dilemmas that the Indian manager is confronted with. These lead to an examination of deep cleavage in the mind and heart of the Indian manager. The chapter builds on the two archetypal symbols of Hema and Ravi to explore these two faces of Indianness and how these manifest in organizations and systems. The chapter makes several references to eminent thinkers and academicians, including Ashis Nandy, Dharampal, Sudhir Kakar and Pulin Garg, leveraging on their insights on the Indian psyche and mind-set.

Chapter 7: leadership polarities and Indian managers

This chapter integrates the EUM framework with leadership, inviting the reader to examine and work with four polarity scales. The chapter brings forth our researched data that reveal that there are preferences of the leader towards each of the scales that reinforce the role proclivity of the Indian leader, in general. Along with individual role preferences, this chapter also offers insights on aspirations as well as how the Indian manager looks at other people. This includes perceptions, judgments and projections and gives a better understanding of how the Indian manager looks at leadership as a process.

This chapter will introduce and deploy four leadership polarities and explore the orientation of Indian managers both as suggested by the statistical data, theoretical formulations and experiential insights.

These polarities are the following:

a   Preservation versus transformation
b   Meritocracy versus humanism
c   Control versus empowerment
d   Objective Rationality versus subjective sensing

Chapter 8: the two perspectives

In the chapter, we would like to offer a framework that not only explores and explains the stance of the Indian manager across four leadership polarities, but in order to deconstruct the two archetypes of Ravi and Hema referred throughout the book, offers two broad perspectives, P1 and P2, that are based on our understanding of human collectives.

The P1 integrates the Homo economicus, the Rational Ingenieur and the agonic mind-set, while P2 integrates the Homo reciprocans, the Bricoleur, and the hedonic mind-set.

The chapter explores how these two perspectives create an inner dissonance within the Indian manager as he or she seeks to live up to P1 as demanded by modernity and yet is aware of the pull of P2 that is influenced by the civilizational codings and culture.

Chapter 9: integrating the two perspectives

This final chapter first focuses on the divergent pulls of the two perspectives as conceptualized in the earlier chapter on the Indian manager today. It stresses the need to integrate the two as opposed to splitting and how this would impact challenges and concerns that manifest both at the individual and the systemic level. It offers an understanding of the challenges that the individual and the system face today, as well as offers ideas and new practices that would bring about the co-holding of P1 and P2.

Some of the key challenges manifesting at the individual level include the exercising of agency and dealing with differences. At the systemic level, the challenges include confronting the preoccupation with only the tangible dimensions of the system, a lack of ownership and a dominant masculinity that brings in stress without any replenishment.

It offers ideas, perspectives and invites the reader to explore new ways of looking at the phenomena when it comes to co-holding P1 and P2.

Notes

1 Rajshri Productions Pvt. Ltd., established in 1947, is a film production company based in Mumbai, India. It has produced several successful films and TV serials that focus on the dramas pertaining to dynamics within Indian joint families.
2 Aristotle, the famous Greek philosopher whose work on rules of logic is known as Organon – a collection of six works on logic compiled in 40 BCE.

Chapter 2

Evolution of EUM

A personal journey

The creation and evolution of EUM have much to do with two interrelated themes – my interest in understanding my cultural identity as an Indian and my unease with frameworks, which classify people into fixed categories. I believe there is some relationship between these two themes, though I only have a hazy idea about what connects them. Like most other urban, middle-class Indians of my generation, my education and cognitive development were primarily through frames, which can broadly be called "Western". On the other hand, the kind of folklore, mythology, music, literature, films, beliefs/values, rituals and practices that I grew up with were largely Indian, and the two didn't always synchronize well.

Viewed through the lens of objective rationality and absolutistic morality, there is no way one could assign "godhood" to someone like Krishna,[1] who stole, teased women, manipulated during the war and so on. To deify his adulterous relationship with Radha seemed ridiculous – and one couldn't even treat it as a pure and symbolic affair because there was Geet Govinda[2] to remind you of their intense physical encounters.

Simultaneously, to regard Rama,[3] who throws out his wife merely on the basis of a rumor, as Maryada Purushottam (or the embodiment of Honor, Dignity and Propriety) made no sense. The difficulty was not just in the realm of mythology but all pervasive. Respecting your elders is fine, but what rational sense do practices like touching their feet or not expressing disagreement make? Wasn't faith healing just a whole lot of mumbo-jumbo, and what was the "scientific" basis of the grandma's so-called traditional wisdom?

On the other hand, cognitive frameworks when looked at from the "emotive" lens created as much difficulty. If one's basic sense of "son-hood" has been shaped by myths of Rama or Shravan Kumar,[4] how do you reconcile with the idea of Oedipus complex?

Similarly, if commitment to Dharma and self-less fulfillment of role obligations is seen as the ideal state, then the very idea of "motivation" seems somewhat repulsive and manipulative. If the belief is that leaders are supposed to inspire and not motivate, then any theory of motivation can at best be appreciated cognitively and will create emotional ambivalence. And what does one do with frameworks like "Management by Objectives" when one has been brought up on the philosophy of Nishkaam Karma (act from conviction rather than worry about consequences).

For a long time, I attributed this tension to binaries like Tradition/ Modernity, Subjective/Objective, Faith /Reason and so on. It was my teacher at Indian Institute of Management, Ahmedabad, Dr. Pulin Garg who opened my eyes to the significance of culture and philosophical underpinnings of any cognitive framework.

In his own words, Pulin[5] said,

> While the manifest contents of individual and organization behaviour can be viewed, analysed and explained by behavioral science concepts developed in the west, the latent contents, the sources and processes underlying manifest behavior cannot be understood. The western behavioral science concepts are quite viable, but they are defined in terms of discrete categories, which often tend to be exclusive of each other. They are very often linear. Indian social and individual reality cannot be subsumed in such kind of categories. Based on studies in history, language and other aspects of Indian culture, it becomes apparent that Indian world is constructed in patterns. AS such "pattern recognition" is essential to find the primary clue to understand the Indian phenomenology. These patterns are often configurations of specific or sets of disparate units of behavior that co-exist in their interconnectedness to some meaning in individual's identity.
>
> (Garg n.d.)

This realization had a significant impact on my thinking; that is, what were hitherto held as universal truths derived on the basis of objective scientific inquiry became culture-specific formulations, which were useful up to a point but could also become oppressive, particularly if their philosophical foundations were not understood.

It became clear that if one wanted to understand the complexity and nuances of the Indian reality, one needed to look for approaches, which are not reductionist and/or based on Aristotelian binaries of either–or. Both these features don't sit too well with what may be called the Indian way. One can try to understand a phenomenon either through isolating it from other variables or through putting it in the larger context and seeing it in relation to another phenomenon. The Indian preference tilts towards the latter approach. Thus, even in Indian medical sciences like Ayurveda, the emphasis is on looking at the body as a "whole" and acknowledging its interrelatedness with the psyche. From a purely rational point of view, it makes no difference as to who is cooking the food and how he or she is feeling, so long as the person has the requisite skill and competence. However, from the Indian point of view the state of mind of the cook and his or her relationship with the people concerned (as also with what is being cooked) is of utmost importance. A direct implication of this is that measuring individual personality traits/competencies becomes a meaningless exercise from the Indian point of view.

Whether a person gets a score of 1 or 10 on a scale of interpersonal competence is not important. The more important questions are how a person is likely to deal with different interpersonal situations and what would be their likely impact. The desirability or undesirability can only be determined by the context.

Similarly, in the Indian way of thinking, the law of contradiction does not play as significant a role as it does in some other cultures. For Indians, truth is multifaceted and thus cannot be captured as this or that. This is best illustrated in the famous story of seven blind men trying to describe an elephant. Each one of them is right and wrong at the same time and, more important, complement each other for arriving at a more comprehensive truth. It can only be regarded as the next level of truth and not as absolute truth. Nothing is absolutely true, and nothing is absolutely false. Every proposition, no matter how preposterous it may seem, carries a grain of truth in it. Thus, what may be regarded as binaries or polarities in other frames are held as complementarities in the Indian frame. A classic example of this is the Indian approach to principles of masculinity and femininity. They are neither mutually exclusive nor two poles of a continuum. Instead, they are complementary to each other. Hence, higher masculinity does not mean lower femininity and vice versa. In fact, it is perfectly possible for an individual to be highly masculine and highly feminine at the same time. This is equally applicable to virtually all binaries such as mind–matter, internal–external, feeling–thinking, rationality–faith, submission–dominance, centrality–marginality and so on.

Beneath this non-reductionist, non-Aristotelian approach lies a fluid definition of the Self. In the Indian frames, Self is not an object but an ever-flowing process. It is more akin to a verb than a noun. At the object level, the Indian approach does not recognize any difference between people or any other form of creation for that matter. The fundamental belief being that all forms of creation are composed of the same basic elements. It is the configuration and interplay of these elements, which makes an individual, species or material forms as distinctive. Objects can be studied by putting them into different categories or types, but a fluid configuration can only be studied through pattern recognition and interplay both within the entity and the dynamics of interaction with the context.

You cannot study a river as an object. You can only understand it in terms of its flow and the terrains through which it passes. Hence, any approach which denies the fluid and dynamic nature of the Self and attempts to understand the Indian reality in terms of tightly defined categories will not be able to capture the complexity and nuances of the individual/collective experience. Through the lens of such frames the individual/collective will only appear as inconsistent, full of contradictions and hypocritical. If one wishes to have a more "empathetic" understanding of the Indian reality, one needs a frame, which resonates with the basic Indian beliefs about human existence and condition.

To a large extent, I found this resonance in Clare Graves's framework of value systems/levels of existence (Graves 1970).[6] When my friend and colleague S. R. Ganesh introduced me to it, I experienced a strong pull towards it.

Some of the features that attracted me were the following:

1   The framework postulated by Graves regarded human nature as ever evolving/emerging and not a set thing.
2   It postulated an evolutionary path, which is shared by all human beings and yet is traversed by each person in his/her unique way.
3   It looked at human psychology in a holistic manner, which included the individual's needs, motivations, beliefs, values and conditions of existence together and in relationship with each other. Thus, the person was not being placed into a prefixed box but being seen in relation to several value systems/existential levels.

Thus, here was a framework that did not study human beings in a piecemeal manner (through needs, traits values, etc.) but looked at the individual as an integrated whole. Simultaneously, it recognized the relationship of the individual with his or her context. It provided for both commonalities of human condition and distinctiveness of the individual's journey. There was acknowledgment of the inherent dynamicity of human beings. Most important, it provided a structure, which was sufficiently fluid to accommodate the uniqueness of the individual.

The next important step was the research, which Ganesh and I undertook on work values of Indian managers. For this, we had used an instrument developed by Scott and Susan Myers,[7] which was based on Graves's framework.

One of the features of this instrument, which appealed to me, was that it did not require the individual to make either–or choices. Instead, the individual was required to distribute 12 points among six different statements for each question. The six statements corresponded with the six levels of Graves's framework.

These six levels are postulated in the following hierarchical order, akin to Maslow's[8] hierarchy of needs:

1   *Tribalistic* (equivalent of UBP in EUM): The prime end value at this level is safety, which is achieved through living according to the ways of one's elders. The individual at this level is strongly influenced by authority and tradition, has low appetite for risk, prefers the familiar and has strong attachment with the context.

2   *Egocentric* (equivalent of USD in EUM): At this level the individual's main needs are self-assertion, adventure and fulfillment of own desires. The primary philosophy is of rugged individualism, survival of the fittest and "might is right".

3   *Conformistic* (equivalent of URB in EUM): The main emphasis at this level is on having a stable interface with the context through well-defined roles, boundaries and expectations. The individual lives by the established rules of the system/norms of appropriateness and expects the same from others.

4   *Manipulative* (equivalent of UPA in EUM): At this level the main emphasis is gaining mastery over one's life, fulfilling one's potential and transcending the limitations of one's context. The individual is driven by a need for achievement, strategic thinking, competency building and goal-directed movement.

5   *Sociocentric* (equivalent of UMI in EUM): At this level the
emphasis is on being a "meaningful part" of the larger context
to which one belongs. The individual is driven by sensitivity,
empathy, harmony, egalitarian outlook and humanistic values.

6   *Existential* (equivalent of UDS in EUM): At this level the
emphasis is on co-holding the multiple and often conflicting
forces both within oneself and in the context. The individual
lives in the "here and now" and relies on contextual wisdom
rather than any final answers.

A more detailed description of the EUM Universes is provided in
the next chapter.

The findings of our research, which were published in the
March 1975 issue of ASCI *Journal of Management*, showed that
the first preference of the managers in our sample was for the sixth
level, that is, Existential values (UDS), followed by the third, that
is, Conformistic (URB); fourth, that is, Manipulative (UPA); fifth,
that is, Sociocentric (UMI), first, that is, Tribalistic (UBP); and the
second, that is, Egocentric (USD) was a distant last.

Table 2.1 summarizes the rankings for the levels of existence.
Clearly, there was a strong influence of normative desirability at
work in Existential being *preferred at* the top level. So, we decided
to dig deeper to look at the specific aspects for which each value
system was being preferred by comparing the relative scores of different elements in each value system.

The results of this endeavor showed a clear bias towards the
Conformistic level. In each level, elements, which were in sync
with the Conformistic level, were scored consistently higher than
those that were not. For example, Sociocentric level was valued

Table 2.1 Preferred ranking of levels in the 1974 research

Values	EUM	Preference
Tribalistic (Level 1)	UBP	Rank 5
Egocentric (Level 2)	USD	Rank 6
Conformistic (Level 3)	URB	Rank 2
Manipulative (Level 4)	UPA	Rank 3
Sociocentric (Level 5)	UMI	Rank 4
Existential (Level 6)	UDS	**Rank 1**

Source: All tables in this book have been prepared by the author out of data
based on his research.

for "organization's responsibility towards people" but shunned for items such as emotionality, sensitivity, warmth and so on. Even in the Existential level, items which conflicted with Conformistic level (such as spontaneity, autonomy, etc.) were valued least. There were many lessons for me from this experience:

1   The value systems were intertwined with each other and studying them in isolation can be misleading.
2   Any evolutionary frame will necessarily create a pull of normative desirability with the higher levels being seen *or deemed* as superior.
3   This normative pull is not of an absolute nature as evidenced by the fact that there was a sharp drop from the first (Tribalistic) to the second (Egocentric) level and a gradual decline from third (Conformistic) to fourth (Manipulative) and fifth (Sociocentric) levels.
4   Cultural identity played a significant role in the way the Indian manager defined his or her systemic membership and role taking; for example, selflessness *is* coupled with exaggerated expectations *of the individual* from the system.

All these learnings were to have a significant impact on my future work. However, at that time it did not go very much beyond a few experiments like developing an instrument on "values for living" more or less on the same lines as the instrument that we had used in our research and attempts to link it with sociometric choices – a project that was abandoned halfway through because of a variety of reasons.

In 1980, I left the academic world and had my first real encounter with the corporate world.

This gave me a firsthand exposure to the world of Indian managers – how they took their roles, how they defined their membership in the system, what were their values, what governed their choices and so on.

When I entered the corporate world, my mental picture of the Indian manager was of a person who had a strong commitment to the system, whose loyalties were personalized, who behaved like a good obedient soldier with the boss and expected the same from his or her subordinates, whose basic model of authority was a benevolent father figure, who liked to be clear about what was expected from him or her, who was uncomfortable with open and direct expression of ambition and aggression, whose demeanor was of self-effacement but who simultaneously expected the system to take care of his or her needs and so on. To a large extent, the experience reinforced this image, but there were many dissonances as well. I found that the commitment of the Indian manager was often less of a choice and more of a compulsion arising out of a sense of insecurity and a lack of choices.

In fact, he or she was quite alienated from the system, and often adherence to systemic discipline arose from a fear of consequences than any real respect for them. In absence of this fear, callous disregard for the system became a norm rather than an exception.

In an article published in *Business India* (Malhotra 1979),[9] I articulated some of these impressions and contrasted them with the findings of the research study done in 1974. My speculation was that over this decade, the situation had changed considerably and if the same study was done now, the results would be quite different.

I was wrong.

The data gathered subsequently (though through a different instrument) showed a pattern very similar to what had been found in 1974. In fact, until as late as 2016, we did not witness any significant departure from the 1974 findings.

It is only in the last couple of years that we may be seeing some shifts, but it is difficult to say how significant they are. What has now become clear in hindsight is that the differences that I found in my experience from the findings of the 1974 study were on account of the *repressed Egocentric level* (USD in EUM) and not on account of any real change in the situation. It is not that the Indian managers had become more egocentric but only that our research could not capture the fact that they tend to project their egocentricity on to others.

The 1974 study had also shown a very low score for the Egocentric level, but because of the limitation of the framework/instrument it could not catch its projection on to others. Just because our respondents did not identify with the Egocentric level, it does not mean that its features did not exist in them – it was merely being repressed by them and being projected on to others. The earlier instrument could not catch this repression/projection but became visible in my real-life experience, as became evident in the findings from the EUM data later.

Thus, the question of how does one capture these repressions and projections became another significant factor in the design and evolution of EUM.

It was only around mid-1990s that I revisited the Graves's framework in a comprehensive manner. The trigger was an invitation by my friend Raghu Ananthanarayanan to work with him in a values workshop for a large group of managers from an Indian business house. I shared the framework and my earlier work with Raghu, and we decided to structure the workshop around it. The same instrument was used, but this time we also worked on individual reports for each participant. The entire experience turned out to be a significant reminder of both the power and the limitations of the framework/instrument. It also opened the possibility of using it for mapping individual identity. Thus, began my endeavor to work on the framework and instrument afresh.

It was also the time when I was working very closely with Ma Foi Management Consultants. Besides being the non-executive Chairman, I was also involved in its

consulting and research and development (R&D) work. This brought me in close contact with K. S. Narendran, Mustafa Moochala, Abhay Phadnis, Vijay Nair and C. S. Mahesh (who was not a Ma Foi employee but had an active consulting relationship with it). All these people, along with Latha Rajan and K. P. Rajan (promoters of Ma Foi), became my playmates and sounding boards for testing different ideas and approaches.

After experimenting with several alternatives, we finally settled on the present instrument. The main factors that went into the design were as follows:

1   No Universe exists in isolation, and hence, the focus should not be on individual Universes but on their interplay – the 15 words represent the intersecting points of the six Universes with each other.
2   The choice of words should be sufficiently open-ended and of a kind that has multiple flavors; for example, the word *Uninhibited* has the flavor of spontaneity as well as recklessness.
3   To the extent possible, the gap between the social desirability of adjectives should be kept to the minimum.
4   Identifying with an attribute and valuing it are two different things and hence the need for separate rankings for Self-Current (SC) and Self-Ideal (SI).
5   How the individual sees him- or herself has a strong relationship with the "group in the mind" that the individual carries and, hence, the ranking of other people (OP).

Consequently, in interpreting the EUM, individual score of a Universe is of less importance. The more important factors include the following:

1   Relative scores in SC, SI and OP
2   Relative scores in each Universe
3   Likely meanings given by the individual to different words

In quick succession, a similar instrument was developed for mapping Organization Identity – on the belief that organizations are living entities and have a distinct character. Empact, a framework for understanding the quality of interface or engagement of the employees with the organization, followed next. All three were intimately connected since they were based on the same philosophical foundation.

This foundation was held more intuitively than clearly articulated. As it happened, around the same time Naren introduced me to the works of Ken Wilber,[10] I found great resonance (and some differences) with many of his ideas. For example, I appreciated his articulation of the 20 tenets of the concept of Holarchy and Holons (Wilber 1995); I did not vibe with the unstated teleological axioms.

Raghu made me aware of the parallel between EUM and the Chakra[11] theory as well as of the influence of Sri Aurobindo on Ken Wilber's work. All this helped me considerably in articulating the foundational beliefs of EUM. Over time, these beliefs have continued to evolve, though they have also maintained a certain continuity.

In this sense, it would be fair to say that EUM is not a product of an a priori comprehensive framework – the framework has its own dynamicity and has been added to/modified with experience.

For nearly a decade and a half, the deployment of EUM was confined to me, Sarbari Gomes and members of Flame Tao. We tried, without much success, to train other people to use the instrument. Several workshops were organized for this purpose. Naren and I also developed a manual that could help in the task of interpretation. While many participants showed great interest in both the framework and the instruments, the actual usage remained limited.

I believe, one of the main reasons for the low actual usage is the inherent complexity of EUM. Thus, it was evident that we needed some way to generate automated reports, which could help the coach/facilitator. However, this was not an easy task. Finally, we managed to a figure out a way of achieving this to a large extent in the two automated reports that we have at present (Coaching and Thematic). Both of them are based on, the principle of picking discrete pieces to create a cogent, individualized picture.

Elements are picked up from different cells and then put together. This enables us to create a unique report for each individual. The total number of permutations and combinations is so huge that it is highly unlikely that any two individuals will get identical reports. The main limitation of these reports is that they neither capture inter-Universe dynamics nor word-pair analysis. These are left to the individual interpreter and the concerned coach/facilitator, *if any*. I hope we will be able to find a reasonably satisfactory solution to this problem in the not-too-distant future. In fact, two other reports (including one on Leadership orientation) which are presently under construction, take care of this limitation, to a great extent.

What continues to excite me about EUM is the possibilities that it offers. This is so because in EUM, the emphasis is not on individual traits, needs, values, levels and so on but on their INTERPLAY. It regards every human being as an interplay between multiple identities and tries to decipher the script of this internal drama and understand the pulls and pushes created by these multiple identities – the harmony and music they try to create as also the conflict and noise which they produce. It is this focus on interplay that fascinates me about EUM.

Notes

1 Krishna is worshiped as the eighth avatar of the god Vishnu. He is a central character in the *Mahabharata*, the *Bhagavata Purana* and the *Bhagavad Gita* and is mentioned in many Hindu philosophical, theological and mythological texts. He is portrayed in various perspectives: a god-child, a prankster, a model lover, a divine hero and as the universal supreme being.

2 Geet Govinda, or the *Song of Govinda*, is a work composed by the 12th-century Indian poet Jayadeva. It describes the relationship between Krishna and the *gopis* (female cow herders) of Vrindavana and, in particular, one gopi named Radha.

3 Rama, also known as Ramachandra, is a major deity of Hinduism. He is the seventh avatar of the god Vishnu. The text of Ramayana – where the entire life story of Rama, Sita (his spouse) and their companions – are allegorically dialogued on to provide the reader with an understanding of duties, rights and social responsibilities of an individual. The text illustrates dharma and dharmic living through model characters.

4 Shravan Kumar epitomizes 'the good son' and is known as a role model for being sincere, respectful, dutiful and loving son, willing to make sacrifices for his blind and aging parents. The poignant story of his short life is embedded in the epic of Ramayana.

5 Garg, P. K. (1989). Cultural identities & their implications for patterns of leadership in Indian organizations. *ISISD- A Primer on Process Work Vol. 1.*

6 Graves, C. W. (1970). Levels of existence: An open system theory of values. *Journal of Humanistic Psychology*, 132.

7 Scott, M. and Myers, S. (1974). Towards understanding the changing work ethic. *California Management Review*, 16(3).

8 Abraham Harold Maslow (April 1, 1908–June 8, 1970) was an American psychologist who was best known for creating Maslow's Hierarchy of Needs, a theory of psychological health predicated on fulfilling innate human needs in priority, culminating in self-actualization.

9 Malhotra, A. (1979, January 14–27). Value erosion and managerial alienation in Indian organizations. *Business India*, p. 79.

10 Ken Wilber, or Kenneth Earl Wilber II (b. January 31, 1949), is an American writer on transpersonal psychology and his own Integral theory. Ken Wilber's work now spans two decades, from *The Atman Project* (1980) to *A Theory of Everything* (2001), and it includes some 20 books. In most of these books Sri Aurobindo's work, especially *The Life Divine* and *The Synthesis of Yoga*, are referenced, and his language of integral transformation and spiritual evolution is frequently used. Wilber is also known for articulating the 20 properties of Holons (Wilber 1995).

11 Chakra theory, sometimes spelled Cakra or Cakka, refers to any center of subtle body, not the physical body, and are believed to be a psychic-energy centers in Indian tradition. The Chakras, as per the traditions of Hinduism, Buddhism and Jainism, are conceived as a series of energy focal points, or psychic nodes that are connected through energy channels called Nadi. The descriptions differ between different schools, but the basic concept is common.

Chapter 3

The **EUM**

Framework and tools

The EUM framework has been inspired by Clare Graves's Open Systems Theory of Values and levels of Existence. The basic premise of Graves, in his own words, is as follows:

1 That man's nature is not a set thing, that it is ever emergent, that it is an open system and not a closed system
2 That man's nature evolves by saccadic, quantum-like jumps from one steady state to another
3 That man's values change from system to system as his total psychology emerges in a new form with each quantum-like jump to a new steady state of being

Graves called these steady states as "Levels of Existence", with each level being a composite system of needs, wants, attitudes, beliefs, values and proclivities that are specific and consistent with internal and external conditions corresponding to that level. Graves posits these levels as an evolutionary hierarchy wherein the individual moves from one level to another, somewhat akin to Maslow's Hierarchy of Needs.

As Graves (1970) puts it,

[t]he psychology of the mature human being is an unfolding or emergent process marked by the progressive subordination of older behavioural systems to newer higher order behavioural systems. The mature man tends normally to change his psychology as the conditions of his existence change. Each successive stage or level is a state of equilibrium through which people pass on the way to other states of equilibrium. When a person is in one of the states of equilibrium, he has a psychology, which

is particular to that state. His acts, feelings, motivations, ethics and values, thoughts and preferences for management are all appropriate to that state. If he were in another state, he would act, feel, think, judge and be motivated in a different manner[1].

On the basis of the preceding framework, Graves postulated eight value systems or levels of existence. However, his research showed that values and behavior of most people were covered by only six levels ranging from the second to the seventh level.

The six value systems postulated by Graves are the main building blocks of EUM. However, in EUM they are called **Universes** and not levels.

There are two main reasons behind this change in nomenclature:

1   Levels are usually associated with superiority/progression, and hence, "higher levels" are regarded as more desirable. As we will see later, the so-called higher levels are neither superior nor inferior. At best, we can see them as states that come later. In order to avoid this association with desirability, we have used the word *Universe* – though in its essence it means the same as what Graves called a value system or an existential level viz. a composite system of needs, beliefs, values, behaviors and so on.

2   The other reason for choosing the word *Universe* is that in our belief, these value systems operate simultaneously and are not chronologically discrete categories. It is not that an individual moves from one level to another but that these Universes reside within an individual and that they awaken in a certain chronological order. By the time an individual reaches adulthood, all the six Universes get awakened though their relative strength, and intensity varies from person to person. Thus, in EUM, each person is regarded as a unique configuration of all the six Universes. The underlying belief is that all human beings are composed of the same elements and that what makes each person unique is the configuration of these elements. This configuration is not static because human beings are naturally dynamic: there are constant transitions and transformations taking place that are both continuous and discontinuous. With each transition/ transformation, the whole reconfigures itself into a reasonably coherent system of values, beliefs, attitudes, and so on.

The EUM framework assumes that, like individuals, organizations, too, are a unique and dynamic configuration of similarities and differences and that their evolution can be studied and understood in a manner similar to that of human beings. In organizations, the configuration expresses itself through the organizational culture.

The EUM suite of tools try to capture clear snapshots of the current reality, possible future movements, dilemmas, potential, action choices, and challenges for both the individual(s) as well as the organization that they are a part of.

The EUM Universes

The EUM Universes are reasonably distinct, and each Universe is coherent in itself, but all the Universes exist in simultaneity: the interplay between them is critical to understanding the uniqueness of the organism and its stresses, dilemmas and potential, among other things.

A brief description of the Universes for the individual and the organization is given in Table 3.1.

The main features associated with these Universes are provided in Appendices 3.1 and 3.2 at the end of this chapter.

As can be seen, there is a close and mutually reinforcing relationship between the individual and organizational Universes. For example, an organization, which is high on the Clan Universe, is likely to encourage a higher UBP orientation amongst its members. Similarly, individuals who are high in USD are likely to create an Arena culture in their organization. This is not to suggest that the two are always in perfect sync with each other, or even should be so.. In fact, too tight an alignment can create entrenchment and stagnation, whereas a loose fit can propel both the individual and the organization toward movement and evolution.

How the EUM works

It is important to remember that although the Universes are explained as distinct and disparate states, they are not mutually exclusive: the EUM considers all the individual Universes to be present in each individual, and all the organizational Universes to be present in each organization.

Table 3.1 Individual and organizational Universes

Individual Universes	Organizational Universes (Cultures)
UBP People whose dominant location is in this Universe are primarily driven by the need for safety and security. They have a high level of comfort with the familiar and the known and prefer to operate from defined patterns and precedents. Preservers of tradition, they are very good at maintaining continuity and anchorage. As leaders, they are dependable and protective but at the same time may expect obedience and loyalty. They are unlikely to be very comfortable with change and people working with them may feel cut off and obsolete in an ever-changing context.	**Clan** In this Universe, the organization culture is focused primarily towards tradition, continuity and a strong sense of belonging to the organization. While this has the benefit of a close-knit familial culture, it creates difficulty in taking risks for progress, working towards change and developing a meritocratic leadership orientation.
USD People in this Universe bring with them all that denotes individualism – creativity, adventure, fun, energy, bravado and heroism. The world is quite polarized and is often labeled as one with haves and have-nots, winners and losers, predators and victims. The individual has a high need for challenges and a burning desire to surmount all odds. There is a difficulty in trusting especially role related authority. Dependency, obedience, submission and so on are looked down upon. As leaders, they are likely to be aggressive – protecting and expanding their turf and sometimes ruthless in the process. They have high demands from themselves and others and not overly concerned about authority figures. People who work with them will feel the rush and excitement of pursuit but also will be prone to feeling anxious and afraid of being exploited.	**Arena** In this Universe, the members of the organization have the propensity to be energetic, competitive and expansive. On one hand, this creates an appetite for risk taking and adventure and, on the other, may reduce the scope of collaboration and cooperation within the organization as well as making the members overtly vigilant towards protecting turf and personal rewards and punishment. The organization culture is oriented more towards "win at any cost" rather than a thought-through and goal-directed strategic objective.

URB

People in this Universe seek a world of order, responsibility and stability. They recognize opposing forces especially between the Self and others and believe in resolution through balance.

They have a high regard for discipline, duty, norms and rules and believe in the rightful exercising of just authority.

As leaders, they take it upon themselves to uphold the sanctity of the system and may be punitive towards deviants. They are encouraging of efficient, orderly execution of role responsibilities but, at the same time, may appear as authoritarian, rigid, dogmatic and absolutistic.

People working with them will experience order and stability but may be prone to suppression of creativity and personal ambition.

UPA

People in this Universe are ambitious but practical. Their goals and targets are based on reality rather than wishful thinking.

They often see the world as a marketplace where each person stakes her or his competence in return for a price.

As leaders, they focus on merit, excellence, learning and a need for mutually beneficial relationships. They strongly believe in individual contribution and shared responsibility.

There does exist, however, a sense of island-hood, discomfort with intangibles and a fear of vulnerabilities. A high sense of performance orientation, task focus and a standard of excellence may result in burnout for themselves as well as for others.

Clockwork

This is a Universe in which the members of the organization seek order and stability and wish to maintain it through rules, policies and structure. The organization is high on predictability, and discipline and low on vibrancy and innovation.

While it provides stability, role clarity and clear goals, it expects adherence to discipline, duty and norms from its members in return. This organization is diligent and demanding yet benevolent and protective.

It would have conventional systems and a hierarchical workplace. This organization will find it difficult to change unless heralded by extreme situations.

Network

In this Universe, the members are motivated by a need for success and achievement. In order to achieve success, members simultaneously compete, collaborate and create relationships that are based on task, link and mutual aspirations.

In this organization task defines power, authority and information requirements. The culture is geared towards meritocracy, continuous learning and a strong bias for action and speed.

The organization is aware of business environments and works with strategy driven goals. This organization is also prone to create burnouts in people and values people only on the basis of their contribution.

(Continued)

Table 3.1 (Continued)

Individual Universes	Organizational Universes (Cultures)
UMI In this Universe, the prime needs are to offer and to connect with others for the sake of relating rather than for a functional, purpose-loaded personal agenda. There is a greater valuing of acceptance and respect for people than merely for achieving success. As leaders, people in this Universe place emphasis on inclusive processes, egalitarian/democratic values and work towards the good of the greater collective. With their participative style of leadership, they will seek consensus and are likely to be uncomfortable with unpleasant realities/tough stances. They may suffer from a possible loss of pragmatism and task focus.	**Ecology** In this Universe, the members of the organization value democracy, inclusiveness and relationships among all 'stakeholders'. This organization works towards inclusivity, listening to all including the marginalized and mentoring individuals. This organization believes that quality of life is more important than career success as an absolute value. The organization has a concern for environmental consequences of systemic actions. Members of the organization are valued both for their abilities as well as for their individual uniqueness and human qualities. On the other hand, absoluteness about the need for inclusivity and democracy can bring in a loss in task focus and can create superficial bonhomie, public agreements and private disagreements, leading to visible and invisible waste.
UDS In this Universe, the commitment of the individual is to live in the here and now. There is implicit acceptance that there are no absolutes in life and that opposites coexist. There is acceptance of multiplicity within oneself as also of differences between people. The emphasis is on dialog rather than elimination of differences. As a leader, the individual can be experienced as extremely inspiring and a visionary who can see the whole picture, face the inherent complexities and dilemmas and use his or her subjective wisdom to exercise contextually meaningful choices. Simultaneously, the individual may be seen as fuzzy, unpredictable, difficult to understand and indecisive.	**Holon** In this Universe, the members learn to value and accept duality. While there is a sanctity of systems and structures, there is a recognition that they cannot be adhered to in an absolute manner in all situations and have to be seen in a context. People in this organization are valued for their competence/ contribution as well as for who they are. Customers are partners with this organization, sharing a stake in the well-being of the organization. This organization values both objective analysis and subjective wisdom. The organization values measurement for learning and not for control. In this Universe, the members honor heritage and yet remain open to new influences.

However, individuals and organizations differ in respect to the following:

- Extent to which they identify with a Universe
- Extent to which they value a Universe
- Extent to which they regard a Universe as a distinguishing feature about themselves

These three dimensions put together create several permutations and combinations. A person may strongly identify with a Universe but may not necessarily value it; for example, a person who identifies with UBP may feel good about being a loyal and committed member of the system OR may experience him- or herself as a captive and feel resentful about it.

Similarly, an organization that identifies strongly with Arena may wish to retain and further enhance its energetic, passionate and unpredictable ways, OR it may wish to bring in a degree of systemic discipline and processes through higher Clockwork orientation.

Again, the identification with a Universe does not necessarily imply that the individual/organization regards it as a distinguishing feature. A person with strong identification with USD may regard it as a special feature (if it is not seen in others) OR may regard it as a normal feature of most human beings (if it is also seen in others) In the first scenario, the individual is likely to take his or her dominant position for granted whereas, in the latter, he or she would be constantly vigilant about potential challenge from others.

There is also the question of feelings associated with the distinctiveness. The person may like the distinctiveness or experience it as a burden. Thus, a person who believes that he or she is more UMI oriented than most other people may feel good about being more empathetic and inclusive OR may feel that this orientation works to his or her disadvantage.

The EUM instruments try to inquire into the unique stance of the individual/organization in respect of each of these Universes as well as map the unique configuration of the six Universes as it exists in the individual/organization at a given point of time.

Finally, health and pathology in this framework are not black-and-white. Indeed, the framework posits that people/organizations need to move through and across *all* the Universes if they are to be fully healthy and effective. Movement between the Universes can be through evocation (propelled by inner awakening) and through provocation (as a coping mechanism from external compulsions);

the former is likely to be healthier since the inner motivation assumes that the organism is ready for the movement.

In sum, the EUM does not categorize an individual/organization in an N × N matrix, nor does it 'tag' the individual/organization for life. EUM focuses on understanding the uniqueness of an individual/organization without classifying 'strengths' and 'weakness' that need to be leveraged or tackled. It sees individuals/organizations as dynamic and with an inherent capacity for change.

The EUM examines the current location of an individual/organization; the possible causes for this and directions/choices for the future, as well as anticipated blocks and impediments. Thus, the individual/organization is sought to be understood in a continuum rather than in a stagnant, 'freeze-frame' observation.

The tools

In its design, the EUM is constructed on the fundamental premise that words have a wide range of meanings rather than a fixed/*unique* meaning. Depending on the individual's/organization's dominant Universe or combination of Universes, it is likely that there will be association and assignment of certain meanings to words rather than certain others.

EUM-I

Simply described, the EUM-I asks an individual to rank order 15 adjectives, and thrice – the test taker's responses (ranking from 1 to 15, with 1 being most descriptive and 15 being least descriptive).

These rankings produce a picture in three parts:

- One's perception of how the Self is currently configured (SC)
- One's idea of the 'ideal' Self (SI)
- One's perception of people in the world at large (OP)

(See Appendix 3.3.) SC shows the extent of identification, SI shows the extent of valuing and OP the extent to which it is seen in others. The difference between SC and OP shows the extent of distinctiveness. Thus, if an individual has a significantly higher score in SC as compared to OP, then it indicates that the individual sees a relatively higher presence of that Universe in Self as compared to others.

On the other hand, if the OP score is higher, then it means that the Universe is seen as more dominant in others than in oneself. The feelings associated with the distinctiveness are indicated by the SI score. If the SI score is closer to SC, then it indicates that the individual is feeling good about the distinctiveness. If SI is closer to OP, then it means that the distinctiveness is being seen as a burden by the individual.

For example, let's take a person who has the following score pattern in the Universe of Strength and Desire (each cell is scored on a scale of 0 to 50):

- SC (The way I see myself):   10
- SI (The way I wish to be):   12
- OP (The way I see other people): 28

The person seems to be saying that other people are much more self-centric than he or she is, as the OP score at 28 is significantly higher than the SC score of 10. Simultaneously, the individual seems to be comfortable with this difference as the SI score remains more or less same as the SC score. However, if the SI score was 25, then our hypothesis would be that the person is not comfortable with the difference and wishes to reduce the gap between Self and Others.

EUM-O

The EUM-O is based on the premise that each organization operates from a unique combination of these existential Universes. This combination gives insights into the proclivities, entrenchments and issues of the organization.

The instrument is designed on the same principles as in case of EUM-I, except that the number of adjectives is 20 as against 15 in case of EUM-I. The participant is required to simply rank order these 20 adjectives that are representative of the style of functioning of an organization.

The participant has to do this rank ordering thrice so as to reflect the following:

- A perception of the current organizational stance (OC)
- An opinion of the 'ideal' organizational stance (OI)
- A perception of 'most other organizations' (MOO)

(See Appendix 3.4.) OC is akin to SC in case of EUM-I, OI to SI and MOO to OP. Their treatment is identical to what has been stated in case of EUM-I.

Ideational foundations

While working with EUM, it is important to keep in mind, the ideational foundations on which it rests.

1. Pluralism

Pluralism is a common word in philosophy and metaphysics, often used in opposition to reductionism and monism and where it is assumed that there is more than one reality and that there is not *one* consistent means of discovering truth but many paths.

The fundamental doctrine of Jainism – which is of Anekantavada[2] (Sanskrit meaning "many-sidedness") rests on the notion that *"reality is perceived differently from diverse points of view, and that no single point of view is the complete truth"*.

The parable of the elephant and the five blind men, each clutching a part of the elephant and yet believing that he knows the true nature of things comes closest to explaining the notion of Anekantavada.

The underlying principle is that **reality** is multifaceted and no finite set of statements can capture the entire truth, and hence, *"all knowledge is at best only provisional and tentative"*.

This principle is at the heart of EUM. As stated earlier, the instrument is designed on the assumption that words do not have one fixed meaning but a wide range of flavors. It is also assumed that within each Universe there is coherence as also tension. For example, in the UBP, for some people the elements of belonging may go hand in hand with elements of protection, just as for many others, belonging may be accompanied by exploitation and oppression rather than safety and protection.

Finally, no individual is seen as operating from only one or two Universes. Thus, it becomes important to look at every phenomenon through the lens of each Universe. For example, when control is seen through the USD, it appears like an issue of personal power, but when it is seen through the URB lens, it becomes an issue of structural legitimacy.

What this implies is that there are no absolute meanings in EUM. By itself, any single score is of very little relevance. In a sense, each score is taken as "one part of the story", and it is only through putting together these pieces, can a reasonably cogent narrative can be built.

Thus, pluralism is ingrained in the design of the instrument, in the way each Universe is conceived, in the interplay between the Universes and in the way an individual profile is interpreted or dialogued on.

The basic attempt in EUM is to trigger an inner dialog between the multiple selves that reside within each one of us. Sometimes these multiple selves cohere with each other, and sometimes they are at loggerheads. In absence of a dialog, we run the risk of either getting caught with a monochromatic view of ourselves and our situation OR take recourse in relativism; that is, all viewpoints are equal; therefore, "anything goes". A dialog opens the possibility of new meanings and action choices.

2. Interactive Universes

The six Universes do not operate in isolation but are in constant interaction with each other. While each Universe is a composite system in itself, it operates in conjunction with other Universes. Thus, it is not uncommon for an individual to seek fulfillment of a need associated with one Universe through a behavior that belongs to another Universe. A typical example is a person becoming aggressive when feeling insecure.

Although, by itself, safety is a UBP need, it can prompt a USD behavior, for example, aggression. Similarly, the fulfillment of a USD need of power through audit/control/boundary management, which are essentially URB behaviors, is fairly common.

The impact of any Universe on the thoughts, feelings and actions of an individual is significantly impacted by other Universes. Thus, a person in whom both USD and UPA are impactful is likely to lead from the front-set direction/strategy, give clear instructions and expect others to follow. On the other hand, a person in whom UPA is dominant but USD is suppressed is likely to lead in a supportive and participative manner.

If USD is dominant and UPA is suppressed, then the person is likely to be intuitive, mercurial and unpredictable in his or her leadership behavior. Thus, no single Universe determines the behavior of the individual by itself. It is always the combination and their interplay. Even in cases where any single Universe is extremely dominant, the relative influence of other Universes has a significant role to play. A high USD has a completely different meaning when supported by moderate UMI and URB as compared to a high USD supported by moderate UPA and UBP. The former is more likely to be an evangelist whereas the latter is more likely to be a mafia don.

Thus, the main focus in EUM is to explore the interplay between the six Universes and certainly not on boxing an individual in any one or two Universes.

3. Perspective on evolution

In line with Graves's thinking, EUM looks at human beings as dynamic and human nature as ever evolving. It also accepts that this evolution follows a certain pattern. However, this evolution is only a phenomenon, and there is nothing desirable or undesirable about it. In common parlance, we tend to regard an "evolved" person as also a more "desirable" person.

This would be akin to saying that a tree is superior to a sapling or a sapling is superior to a seed. Just because a state of being is preceded by another state of being, it does not necessarily become better or worse. A telling example of this is the Indian notion of Yugas.[3] According to this framework, "*Kaliyuga*" (the present-day times) is the most "evolved" yuga, and yet in popular understanding, it is held as the "worst". It is to avoid this association with normative superiority that we have opted for the more neutral term *Universe* than a value-laden term *Level*.

The notion of normative hierarchy is reinforced by the fact that most evolutionary frameworks including Maslow's, have an implicit or explicit 'teleology'. Hence, it is important to differentiate evolution from teleology, for EUM is an evolutionary framework but not necessarily a teleological one.

Teleology (from Greek *telos*, meaning "end" or "purpose") is the philosophical study of nature by attempting to describe things in terms of their apparent *purpose* or a *goal*. The philosophy contends that all entities including systems evolve towards this 'purpose'. As a consequence, a grand narrative is either expressed or assumed, and an active and conscious pursuit of this purpose is glorified

In EUM, evolution is regarded as a natural process – which does not necessarily have an intent, a purpose or rational planning behind it. It is just a process obeying the laws of the Universe. We can have different opinions on whether this evolution has a purpose, but the fact of evolution itself cannot be denied.

Assigning "intent" or "purpose" to evolution is akin to shooting an arrow blind into the darkness and uncertainty of future and then painting a target around it after it has landed – this kind of 'hindsighting' process takes us away from understanding evolution. For example, giraffes did not *plan* to evolve long necks, and birds did not *choose* to evolve wings – this just happened after millions of years to survive.

An important implication of the nonteleological approach to evolution is that in EUM, the earlier Universes, particularly UBP and USD, are treated as the foundation of an individual's identity. Each Universe is treated as a significant learning opportunity for the person with its own unique learning agenda. For example, in UBP, the individual learns how to trust and belong. The major learning agenda in USD is acknowledging one's own needs, discovering potency and learning to assert. URB teaches how to relate to systems, adherence to systemic boundaries, exercising structural authority and so on. In UPA the individual learns how to transcend his or her own and contextual limitations through forging mutually beneficial relationships. In UMI the emphasis is on sensitivity and compassion towards other human beings/ other forms of life and working towards collective well-being. Finally, in UDS, the individual learns to co-hold seemingly opposite forces and face the dilemmas that are an inevitable part of human existence.

Thus, the assimilation of learnings from the preceding Universe(s) has a profound impact on how the individual would engage with the subsequent Universes. A person who experiences failed dependency in UBP is likely to overemphasize the elements of mistrust, counter-dependence and reactivity, among others, in his or her engagement with USD. On the other hand, the individual who has assimilated the learnings of trusting and belonging of UBP will engage with the aspects of playfulness and adventure in USD.

More important, unresolved themes and dilemmas of the earlier Universes impact the individual's integration of the subsequent Universes within.

For example, there could be an individual who has low UBP scores and high URB and UPA scores. In a teleological framework, such a person will be seen as someone who has "transcended" the need for "safety and belonging" and is now operating from a need for "order and achievement". However, while EUM will recognize the propensity of the individual for effective role taking in systems, it will also raise questions about the fatigue that this person may be carrying and the difficulties that he or she may experience in engaging with the sentient aspects of the system.

In other words, in EUM there is no great virtue in being at a higher level (a later Universe) if one has not assimilated the learnings of earlier Universes. A classic example of such a phenomenon would be a person who operates primarily from UDS but has not learned the lessons of earlier Universes. Such a person is more likely to get immobilized in face of dilemmas or make expedient choices, rather than face them squarely. In other words, transcendence without inclusion is suppression/repression and not evolution.

4. Part and whole

The term *Holon* was coined by Arthur Koestler (1967),[4] and it means something that is both *whole in itself and a part of another whole*. In this sense, everything can be regarded as a Holon, including material, living and abstract entities.

Thus, an atom is whole in itself but is also a part of a molecule, which, in turn, is part of a cell, and so on.

Similarly, letters of the alphabet are whole in themselves, but are also a part of words, which in turn are part of a sentence and so on. This, of course, does not mean that the molecule is either superior or inferior to an atom. It only represents an increased level of wholeness and complexity. In fact, this increase in the level of wholeness only increases the dependence of the Holon on its constituents.

A typical example of this is, that a hypothetical destruction of all books in the world will not require destruction of all words or alphabets. On the other hand, if all alphabets are destroyed, no words or books can exist. Similarly, human life can exist only if other forms of life exist whereas these other forms (plants, animals, etc.) do not require human beings for their existence.

Furthermore, all holons strive to preserve their identity and autonomy (wholeness) but simultaneously try to become a part of a larger whole. This is equally applicable to human beings. We all wish to be autonomous and fulfill our personal needs, desires and ambitions. Simultaneously, we belong to families, communities, organizations, human species and an ecological order. We try to find a meaningful place for ourselves in these larger "wholes" to which we belong and contribute to them.

Both our wholeness and part-hood create satisfaction as also restlessness. When we operate from our "part-hood", we experience a

sense of belonging, order and meaningfulness, but it can also generate a feeling of suffocation and victimhood (If I am not for myself,
then who will be?).

On the other hand, our "wholeness" gives us a sense of freedom,
potency and mastery over our life, but it can also leave us feeling isolated, lonely, uncared for and meaningless (If I am only for
myself then what's the meaning of my life?).

Thus, the oscillation between wholeness and part-hood is an
inevitable part of human existence. This duality is played out in the
EUM framework.

The six EUM Universes can be seen as a spiral, as shown in
Figure 3.1.

On one side of the spiral are the Universes that lean more on the
side of part-hood (UBP, URB and UMI).

The other side of the spiral has Universes that lean towards
wholeness (USD and UPA).

The sixth Universe, UDS, represents the co-holding of this duality. In UBP, URB and UMI, the individual is focused upon the larger
whole to which he or she belongs – family, clan, community, organization and so on. In USD and UPA, the individual's concern is with
own needs, desires, potency, ambition and so on.

The emergence of these Universes oscillates between the two
sides – part, whole, part, whole, part and finally part and whole
together. The spiral also represents the shortening of the distance
between the two sides as the movement takes place. Thus, USD is
largely governed by the principle of wholeness, but in UPA there
is much higher integration of part-hood. Similarly, UBP is largely

The Evolution Spiral

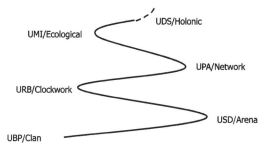

Figure 3.1 Spiral of six EUM Universes

focused on part-hood, but in URB and UMI, there is space for wholeness as well.

5. Self and situation

Another significant aspect of EUM is that it looks at human behavior as a function of both Self and situation, following Kurt Lewin's (1936)[5] heuristic formula, or equation, $B = f(P, E)$.

It therefore follows that one cannot understand the individual in isolation. It is important to know not just how the individual looks at him- or herself but also how the individual looks at his or her situation. An individual who believes that he or she is surrounded by people who are fair and dependable will operate very differently as compared to an individual who believes that other people are not trustworthy. In fact, what a person thinks of others tell us a lot about the person him- or herself. Similarly, what a person thinks of him- or herself may be vastly different from what other people think of him or her.

Thus, we can understand an individual in four basic ways arising from a simple 2 × 2 matrix, as depicted in Figure 3.2, that looks at WHAT is seen, and the LOCATION from which it is seen.

When the location of the viewer is inside and the gaze is internal, what we get is the self-concept of the individual, that is, the way the individual sees him- or herself.

When the location is inside but the gaze is external, what we get is the worldview of the individual, that is, the way the person looks at other people.

Object of View Location Of Observer	Internal	External
Inside	SELF CONCEPT	WORLD VIEW
Outside	IMAGE	CONTEXT

Figure 3.2 Four basic ways of understanding an individual

When the person is seen from an external location, what we get is the image of the person, that is, how the individual is seen by other people.

Finally, the external/outside quadrant pertains to the context of the individual, that is, the attitudes, values, beliefs, preferences, predispositions and so on that are prevalent in the relevant reference group of the individual.

There are both consonances and dissonances across the four quadrants. Thus, the individual's self-concept (internal, inside) and worldview (internal, outside) may be congruous with each other or may clash with each other.

Both consonances and dissonances are critical to understanding the uniqueness of the individual. For example, having a warrior image of oneself will be consonant with the world being seen as a hostile place, whereas it will be dissonant with a peaceful, benevolent perception of the world – each tells a story in its own right, and neither is healthy or unhealthy by itself. Indeed, complete alignment across all four quadrants can lead to entrenchment while dissonances can provide the energy for movement.

Take, for example, the case of an individual whose UBP scores are high in both SC and OP i.e., the individual believes that he/she, as also other people are primarily governed by the need for safety and belonging. If this person also experiences his or her organization as high on Clan, then the person will feel completely aligned with the context. and it is very unlikely that he or she would feel any pressure to make any shift. However, if the same person finds him- or herself in a context that is high on USD and/or Arena, then the person will feel a lack of alignment and will be forced to ask some questions of him- or herself.

6. Identification and distinctiveness

We all look at ourselves in relation to a "reference group". We may identify with this group and/or may feel distinct from it, but it is ever present in the form of a Macro Thou or a generalized picture of the "other" with which we compare and contrast ourselves.

Sometimes our picture of this 'Macro Thou' is conveyed through expressions like "human nature," though we ourselves may not identify with that picture. Thus, it is not uncommon for people to talk of "human nature" in a manner that it excludes them personally. Paradoxically, when we make statements like "Human beings are only governed by self-interest", we may not necessarily identify with that statement. In other words, to a lesser or larger extent, every person is also an exception, at least in his or her own eyes.

Simply put, identification and distinctiveness are two basic processes by which an individual defines him- or herself. Furthermore, both processes are accompanied by feeling tonalities:

- A person may like the fact that he or she is more expressive and forthright as compared to others OR may feel burdened by this distinctiveness.
- Similarly, a person may derive a sense of comfort from being similar to others whereas to another person it may be a source of anguish that he or she, too, is "just like others".

Therefore, in EUM, the attempt is to capture this interplay between what the individual identifies with and what the individual feels distinctive about and the feelings associated with them. This translates into four basic questions which EUM grapples with.

These are the following:

1   Who or what does the person identify with?
2   What does the person regard as distinctive about him or her?
3   How does the individual feel about these identifications and differences"?
4   How is this configuration likely to play out in meaning making, role taking and choice making?

7. Light and shadow

As stated earlier, all six Universes reside in each of us. However, the degree to which they are illuminated, acknowledged and owned up by us varies.

Thus, for someone it may be easier to identify with UBP and URB, and relatively difficult to accept USD, while another person may feel comfortable in UPA but may find it difficult to engage with UBP. The permutations and combinations are immense, and each person has his or her unique configuration of relative illumination/ prominence of the six Universes.

Just because we tend to repress/suppress some of the Universes, they don't cease to exist. They remain in the background and cast their shadow on the Universes, which are in the foreground. Passive aggression is a typical example of this phenomenon. An individual who strongly identifies with UBP and finds it difficult to own up to USD is unlikely to express his or her aggression directly and would tend to discharge it in an insidious manner like sulking, backbiting, silent sabotage and so on. Similarly, an individual who represses/ suppresses UBP but is comfortable with USD is likely to demand absolute loyalty and devotion without actually admitting his or her need for the other person.

Since UBP and USD are the two basic Universes, they are most prone to being suppressed and repressed. Consequently, all the unfinished business of these Universes shows up as shadows in the later Universes.

In conclusion

The essence of EUM is in *interplay*.

It does not box an individual into a category or a type. Instead, it endeavors to the map the interplay, which goes on within each of us. The interplay could be between being a part and a whole, it could be between light and shadow, it could be between identification and distinctiveness, it could be between Self and situation or it can be within the six Universes. The most fundamental assumption in EUM is that there is a continuous inner drama going on within each person.

There are an infinite number of actors involved in this inner drama, but for sake of simplicity, we have reduced them to six. Strictly speaking, the sixth (UDS) is part actor and part "Sutrad-har",[6] who has the additional task of both orchestrating the actors as also connecting with the larger audience, that is, the world at large. This is not to suggest that the Sutradhar is always "in charge" – in fact, most times he or she is not. It is the dynamics among the actors (which includes the Sutradhar), as well as the larger audience, that takes the script forward as the drama unfolds.

Description of EUM-1 Universes

Universe 1

UBP

Nature of this Universe

This is the part of us that wishes to belong to a safe haven where we feel secure and protected. Its primary orientation is towards familiarity, predictability, harmony and strong bonding/identification with our own kith and kin.

It enables us to have trust and faith in our people, abide by the established norms and customs and experience a sense of pride in our heritage. It gives us a strong sense of "oneness" with the group(s) we belong to and enables us to accept all its positives as also its angularities.

When this orientation is subdued, it leaves us feeling rootless and not having a sense of "home". On the other hand, when this orientation is excessive in us, it generates a fear of the unknown, mistrust of "outsiders" and fear of disturbance. Consequently, we become closed to new experience/learning and hence become somewhat like a "frog in the well".

Basic features of UBP

- Basic need for safety and belonging;
- Learning to have trust and faith and to belong;
- High on sincerity and dependability;
- Being content with what one has – accepting the limitations of Self/context;
- Strong sense of anchorage in one's context;

- Comfort with familiar and known – respect for tradition, preserving folklore;
- Willingness to sacrifice for the larger good;
- Repetitive patterns of living;
- Staying within the givens;
- Clinging to "what has always been";
- Sticking together for mutual protection;
- Sticking together for mutual protection;
- Attachment to places and things;
- Deference to power/status/age;
- Way to ensure safety is to "appease the Gods" – totem, magic, superstition, oversimplistic explanations of phenomena, often attributed to the mystical and the magical.

Universe 2

USD

Nature of this Universe

This is the part of us that is focused on fulfillment of our desires and seeks to do so through our own strength and power. Its primary orientation is towards curiosity, assertion, adventure, aliveness, excitement and competitiveness. It enables us to dream for ourselves, invest in developing our strength and power, question the established ways of our context, venture out in the world, undertake heroic journeys, expand our horizons and have a sense of dominance over the world.

When this orientation is subdued, it becomes difficult for us to identify our needs and wishes, assert our own position, engage with conflict/aggression and have self-belief. On the other hand, when this orientation is excessive, we tend to look at other people either as potential enemies to be conquered or as objects for our need fulfillment/self-aggrandizement. It also gives us an unrealistic and exaggerated idea of our strength and may leave us unwilling to acknowledge our vulnerabilities and limitations.

Features of USD

- Basic need is for power and distinctiveness;
- Discovery of one's potency, desire, heroic potential;
- High energy, spontaneity and potential for creative expression;

- Propensity to question the established ways;
- Energized by a sense of challenge;
- propensity to convert encounters into contests;
- Energized by the call of adventure – venturing into the unknown;
- Authority is to be first tested and not blindly trusted;
- "What I desire, I must have NOW" – "All or None"; "Now or Never, My way or the highway";
- Strong urge to express without concern for consequences;
- Competitiveness with a desire to dominate;
- Asserting personal opinions as facts – "My knowing is the only truth";
- Public presentation of prowess and privately held vulnerability;
- Heightened vigilance towards the environment;
- Arrogating victories and successes to the Self and projecting failures and setbacks to others.

Universe 3

URB

Nature of this Universe

This is the part of us that wishes to relate with the world in an orderly fashion so that we know what exactly to expect from others and what is expected of us. Its primary orientation is towards smooth functioning, balance, clarity, adjustment and appropriateness. It enables us to have a sense of proportion, to respect other people's boundaries while protecting our own and to be able to look at situations without getting influenced by our feelings and prejudices. It also enables us to accept that our lives are intertwined with other people's lives, and it is only when each of us performs his or her appointed role in an appropriate manner that we can peacefully coexist.

Thus, in this Universe we attempt to work out appropriate systems and processes to deal with different situations, instill in ourselves and in others a sense of discipline and ensure adherence to mutually agreed-on rules, norms and systems.

When this orientation is subdued, it becomes difficult for us to adhere to any systemic discipline, and all rules and regulations appear to be unnecessary impediments. On the other hand, when this orientation is excessive, we become sticklers for rules, dogmatic, rigid, overcontrolling, inhibited in our expression and intolerant of any deviance/alternative perspectives.

Features of URB

- Basic need for order and stability
- Strong concern for relevance and appropriateness
- Driven by structure, role emphasis and conformity
- Focus on principles, values, norms and established rules and regulations
- Denial of self-needs in the present – in the hope of rewards later
- Recognition of opposites (particularly between Self and others) – resolution through balance
- Aversion to extremes – acceptance of individual orientation/ preference up to an extent
- Reigning in impulses and placing Self in a context
- Self-regulation, role appropriateness, and curbing of spontaneity
- Sharp difference between Self and role
- Going by the letter of the law, playing by the book
- Sharp delineation of spaces
- Bounded adventurism
- Truth is what the book says

Universe 4

UPA

Nature of this Universe

This is the part of us that continually strives towards higher levels of achievement and recognizes that this is possible only by forging mutually beneficial links with others. Its primary orientation is towards purposiveness, goal-directed action, enlightened self-interest and resourcefulness. It enables us to invest in our own capabilities as also respect the capabilities/resourcefulness of others in a way that it can help us to accomplish our goals. Who the other is and what we feel about him or her become less important than what he or she brings to the table. Simultaneously, it makes us recognize that the world values us not for who we are but what we have to offer. Finally, it helps us to relate with others both in a collaborative and competitive manner.

When this orientation is subdued, we experience a sense of drift, self-waste and aimlessness. It also becomes difficult for us to own up our ambitions and/or work towards their fulfillment. When this part is overly dominant, it makes us look at others (as also ourselves) only as instruments of performance/utility and hence feel an inner isolation, loss of human touch, expression of joys and sorrows, fear of obsolescence, feeling burnt out and being in a constant state of "overdrive".

Features of UPA

- Enlightened self-interest
- Appreciation of mutuality of needs – belief in win–win situations
- Future focused – belief in meritocratic culture and investment in building skills, competencies and knowledge
- Goal directed, action oriented, task and strategy focused
- Willingness to postpone/rein in need for immediate self-gratification for long-term benefits
- Achievement defined by "success" and measured through material wealth/social recognition
- Valuing of "tangibles" as the only reality
- Emphasis on outputs and a performance-driven culture
- Preoccupation with increasing one's market value – consequently consumed by fear of failure/obsolescence
- Treating oneself and others primarily as instruments of performance
- Transactional relationships – hence, island-hood
- Ability to make discriminant choices that further goal accomplishment
- Truth is that which is supported by tangible evidence

Universe 5

UMI

Nature of this Universe

This is the part of us that wishes for and works towards a utopian world where everyone can live in peace and harmony. Its primary orientation is towards meaningfulness, intimacy, compassion, empathy and respect for others irrespective of their clan and creed.

It enables us to feel one with the larger human context, transcend the preoccupations of ourselves/our subgroup(s) and dream collectively for a world that ensures a higher level of well-being for all. It also helps us to accept others and ourselves at a human level beyond issues of class, category, ethnicity and so on.

When this orientation is subdued we experience ourselves as self-absorbed, devoid of empathy and compassion, overly consumptive, dry and alone. On the other hand, when it is excessive, we become impractical and are unable to accept that strife is as important for human existence as is harmony.

Consequently, our tolerance for anything that disrupts our idyllic scenario becomes low, and we wish to either ignore it or suppress it.

Features of UMI

- Basic need for meaningfulness and relatedness
- Quality of life held as a primary value
- Self-reflexivity valued
- Interest of the larger collective is valued over Self/own group interest
- Search for synergy – joy of togetherness
- Valuing of acceptance and respect for each other
- Instrumentality of Self/others abhorred/rejected
- Emphasis on collective processes – egalitarian/democratic/inclusive values
- Emphasis on shared resources, community and consensus
- Possible loss of pragmatism
- Discomfort with unpleasant realities
- Reflection is focused internally
- Action orientation coupled with righteousness of a position that is often unexamined

Universe 6

UDS

Nature of this Universe

There are several parts of us that are often at play simultaneously. While they may blend in perfect harmony at times, at other times they may also create severe conflicts and pull us in different directions. Thus, our need for harmony may come in the way of our need for achievement, or our need for dominance may come in the way of our need for intimacy, or our need for safety may come in the way of our need for adventure. The list is endless.

Simultaneous engagement with these multiple pulls is the essence of this Universe. Its primary orientation is towards being in the "here and now", accepting all the different aspects of human existence without judgment and acting on the basis of what seems right in any given situation. It enables us to live with uncertainty, ambiguity and seemingly contradictory pulls without letting one aspect overwhelm the other.

When this orientation is subdued, it makes it difficult for us to live with the inherent uncertainties and ambiguities of life. We tend to become excessively preoccupied either with the past or with the future and are unable to engage fully with the present. Simultaneously, we may become unifocal and start seeking refuges in achievement, in relationships, in power, in knowledge or even in the idea of God. On the other hand, when this orientation is excessive, it can come in the way of our experiencing the various parts of ourselves in their full intensity. It can also become an escape route from the need to take clear positions and making commitments.

Features of UDS

- Simultaneity of Self and system
- Acceptance of multiplicity of the Self
- Engagement with simultaneous pulls from the Self
- Acceptance of all the different aspects of human existence without judgment
- Willingness to engage with uncertainty and ambiguity
- Contextual responses
- Emphasis on 'here and now'
- Accepting that there are no final answers and ultimate refuges
- Deep convictions coupled with an explorative stance – acting on the basis of what feels right
- Equal valuing of expression and relatedness;
- Anchorage without compulsivity;
- Emphasis on flow rather than fight, flight or feign

Description of
EUM-O Universes

Universe I

CLAN

Nature of this Universe

All human collectives, including work organizations, provide a sense of belonging and safety to their members. They play a significant role in our notions about who we are and what are the reference groups to which we belong. Over time, every collective evolves its own set of traditions, norms of behavior and ways of working which it seeks to perpetuate.

In absence of this Universe, a system will have no distinct identity of its own, nor will it be able to forge any emotive link between its members. However, when this Universe is overly engaged with, the system becomes closed to new inputs, ideas and experiences and is unable to keep pace with the ever-changing context.

Main features of clan culture

- Fosters a context of belonging, trust, safety and tradition
- Strongly anchored in respect for heritage and values of continuity
- Places implicit trust in authority and respect for age and experience
- Values harmony/ambience and may seek to sidestep contentious issues
- Live by the "givens" of the past – governed by custom and precedent
- Limited questioning and challenge, premium on obedience, loyalty and selflessness

- Not very proactive in engagement with clients.
- Brand is more in name than a lived reality
- Closed doors policy, will interact only if critical
- Slow to change
- Mentality of parsimony, even when in abundance

Universe 2

Arena

Nature of this Universe

Human collectives are also governed by the principle of "survival of the fittest". This applies both to their internal functioning as well as to their external interface with customers, competitors and other such agencies. Externally, they have to be quick to sense opportunities and threats and act speedily to maximize their own gains. Similarly, internally they have to ensure that, the organization provides opportunities to its members to showcase their strengths and energy as also fulfill their own needs and desires.

When this Universe is subdued, the organization loses its vibrancy and ability to respond quickly and decisively. On the other hand, when this Universe is overly dominant, it creates chaos, arbitrary action, lack of focus, difficulty to collaborate and a sense of insecurity among members.

Main features of arena culture

- Creates a context for adventure and heroic action
- Fosters self-reliance, dynamism, risk taking, pride and self-belief in individuals and groups
- Encourages high energy, spontaneity and potential for creative expression as well as competition – creates winners and losers, powerful and the weak
- A lot of questioning of givens and testing of systemic boundaries – low trust levels
- Aggressive, street smart, opportunistic
- Customer is to be wooed at any cost
- Brand – an asset for short-term gains
- Strong lure of the new with low perseverance
- Resource is viewed as scarce, hence grab
- High vigilance and scanning of environment

Universe 3

Clockwork

Nature of this Universe

All systems need to provide a degree of predictability both to external stakeholders and their own members. This is achieved through laying down rules and regulations, systems and procedures and defining roles and job specifications. It is important that each person knows clearly what is expected of him or her and what he or she can expect from other people and the system.

When this orientation is subdued, the system becomes erratic, chaotic and unpredictable. On the other hand, when this Universe is overly engaged with, the system falls into a monotonous routine and loses its nimbleness, its ability to respond to the "unexpected" and its ability to act swiftly.

Main features of clockwork culture

- 'The Golden Mean' – aversion to extremes
- Provides for clarity, predictability, orderliness – low tolerance for deviance
- Authority is a function of one's position in the hierarchy
- Emphasis on role boundaries and clarity of expectations
- Boundaries are tightly defined, functions are silos, procedure = process
- Incremental improvement
- Values 'objectivity' and blind to subjective sense making
- Project solidity and respectability
- High on efficiency and discipline, low on vibrancy and innovation
- Basic model of engagement: value for money and sanctity of contract
- Brand is a stamp
- Calculated risk (analysis paralysis)

Universe 4

Network

Nature of this Universe

Human collectives are formed and held together through pursuance of goals and aspirations. These goals and aspirations belong to individual members and to the collective as a whole. In this sense, each member can be seen as an autonomous node that is connected to multiple other nodes in a network of mutually beneficial relationships. In order to ensure an effective pursuit of these goals, the organization needs to invest into goal alignment, competence building, continuous learning and creating a culture of meritocracy.

When this orientation is subdued, the members feel underutilized and experience stagnation and a lack of opportunity for advancement. Simultaneously, the system begins to lose its competitive edge. On the other hand, when this orientation is overly dominant, it manifests through feelings of instrumentality, burnouts, fear of obsolescence and ennui.

Main features of network culture

- Emphasis on "what you bring to the table" rather than "who you are" and "where you come from"
- People are seen as bundles of competence and instruments of performance, hence low tolerance for intangibles and subjective reality
- Constantly seeks opportunities for mutual benefit: win–win, invests in customers
- Methods and protocols are used as enabling platform, and not seen as constraining
- Task is what defines power, authority and information requirements
- Fosters throughput orientation, link responsibility, teamwork and collaboration for task performance
- Strong bias for action and speed
- Fear of obsolescence
- Aware of business environment and, often, at the forefront of technology
- Brand is a competitive advantage
- Maximizes profits but does not mortgage the future
- Values climate but not culture – emphasis on interface management

Universe 5

Ecological

Nature of this Universe

Human collectives are also formed for the pursuit of dreams and ideals. These manifest themselves in the form of a mission to contribute to the larger environment rather than treating it only as a source from which one extracts and, hence, only a place of opportunities and threats. Membership in such systems is governed by intimacy and relatedness between soul mates who have shared ideals and humanistic values.

When this orientation is subdued, systems become only a dry landscape of performance and consumption without a larger purpose and meaningfulness. On the other hand, when this orientation becomes overly dominant, it leads to a utopian worldview, a loss of pragmatism and an inability to deal with not so pleasant aspects of human existence like selfishness, jealousy, hatred and so on.

Main features of ecological culture

- Fosters high degree of belonging and ownership
- Values of democracy, inclusiveness and pluralism
- Emphasis on relationships with all stakeholders
- Interdependence not just for task needs but also for human beings
- Invokes not just interdependence of Self and system but Self, system and the larger context
- Human and instrumental side of people celebrated
- Valuing of differences and diversity
- Brand is an expression of idealism
- Aware of environment but guided by inner beliefs and convictions
- Concern for environmental consequences of systemic actions
- Work–life balance emphasized
- Can get carried away by a wave of romantic idealism
- In deifying the "we", the "I" gets lost

Universe 6

Holonic

Nature of this Universe

In every organization, there are multiple forces at play, which sometimes converge and sometimes conflict with each other. Thus, the need of people to belong and relate intimately with each other, can help in goal accomplishment, just as it can come in the way of creating a meritocratic culture. The organization and its members have to learn to manage the inherent tension and accept that there are no final and absolute answers. The main thrust in this Universe is to be in the "here and now" and exercise contextual wisdom to engage with these multiple forces without taking recourse to expediency.

When this orientation is low, the system loses its ability to deal with fluidity, ambiguity and uncertainty. When this Universe is overly dominant, especially if the earlier Universes have not been adequately integrated, the organization can become too fuzzy and unmindful of the need for clarity and certainty.

Main features of holonic culture

- 'Simultaneity' – acceptance of duality
- Dignity of the individual cherished – authentic encounter
- Strong sense of mission permeates everyday action
- Customers are partners – shared stake in well-being of each other
- Value centered but not absolutist – freedom from compulsivity
- Courage to walk alone and pay the price for its convictions
- Values both objective analysis and subjective wisdom
- Brand is a statement of identity
- Values measurement for learning, not control
- Learns from successes and failures, embraces transience and heritage
- "Can make a difference" attitude

The EUM-I instrument

Version I

Instructions

In the page that follows are 15 words. Alongside the column having these 15 descriptive words are three blank columns, A, B and C.

In Column A, you are required to assign a rank to each of the words based on the extent to which these words *describe you*. Thus, if the word "emotional" best describes you, you will assign a rank of 1. If "uninhibited" is the next word that comes closest to describing you, you will assign a rank of 2. You will thus have to rank order all the words from 1 to 15, where 1 best describes how you see yourself and 15 the least.

Column A is thus a portrait of how you see yourself currently.

In Column B, you are required to similarly rank order the 15 words in terms of how you *would like to see* yourself (or how you would wish to be) by assigning 1 to the adjective you would *like to best describe you*, 2 to the adjective you would like *next best* to describe you, and so on.

In Column C, you are required to similarly rank order the 15 words in terms of how you believe *people, in general are* by assigning 1 to the adjective you believe best describes them, 2 to the adjective that *next best* describes them, and so on.

Ensure that all the words carry a rank. Also ensure that no two words carry the same rank.

Please remember that there are no right or wrong answers. Be honest.

This exercise should not take you more than 10–12 minutes.

EMU-I

	A	B	C
	Self – Current	*Self – Ideal*	*Other People*

Rational
Sacrificing
Gracious
Cautious
Emotional
Competitive
Sympathetic
Uninhibited
Collaborative
Dutiful
Fair
Tactful
Tough
Dynamic
Steady

Name	Age
Sex	Department/Function
Total work	Present role
experience	
Qualifications	Email

The EUM-O instrument

Version I

Instructions

In the page that follows are 20 words. Alongside the column having these 20 descriptive words are three blank columns, A, B and C.

In column A, you are required to assign a rank to each of the words based on the extent to which these words *describe your organization*. Thus, if the word "flexible" best describes it, you will assign a rank of 1. If "diligent" is the next word that comes closest to describing your organization, you will assign a rank of 2. You will thus have to rank order all the words from 1 to 20, where 1 best describes how you see your organization and 20 the least.

Column A is thus a portrait of how you see your organization currently.

In Column B, you are required to rank order the 20 words in terms of how you would like to see your organization (or how you would wish it to be) by assigning rank 1 to the adjective you would like to best describe your organization, rank 2 to the adjective you would like next best to describe your organization, and so on.

Column B is thus a portrait of how you would like to see your organization.

In column C, you are required to similarly rank order the 20 words in terms of how you think most organizations, in general are, by assigning rank 1 to the adjective you believe best describes them, rank 2 to the adjective that next best describes them, and so on.

All columns need to be filled in. Ensure that all the words carry a rank. Also ensure that no two words carry the same rank.

Please remember that there are no right or wrong answers. Be honest.

This exercise should not take you more than 20–30 minutes.

EUM-O

	A	B	C
	Organization current	Organization – Ideal	Most organizations
Flexible			
Collaborative			
Efficient			
Hierarchical			
Benevolent			
Strategic			
Ethical			
Informal			
Caring			
Diligent			
Empowering			
Personalized			
Decisive			
Creative			
Expedient			
Demanding			
Diplomatic			
Ambitious			
Protective			
Disciplined			

Background information

Name	Age
Sex	Department/Function
Total work experience	Current role
Tenure in current organization	Qualifications

Notes

1 Graves, C.W. Levels of Existence- an open system theory of values. Journal of Humanistic Psychology. 1970, 10 (2) pp. 131–55.

2 *Anekāntavāda* means "non-absolutism". Anekantavada is one of the basic principles of Jainism that encourages acceptance of relativism and pluralism. According to this doctrine, truth and reality are perceived differently from different points of view, and no single point of view is the complete truth. The word *anekāntavāda* is a compound of two Sanskrit words: *Anekānta*, "manifoldness", and *vāda*, "school of thought". Jain doctrine states that objects have infinite modes of existence and qualities, so they cannot be completely grasped in all aspects and manifestations by finite human perception. Consequently, no specific human view can claim to represent the absolute truth.

3 Yuga in Hinduism is an epoch or era within a four-age cycle. A complete Yuga starts with the *Satya Yuga*, via *Treta Yuga* and *Dvapara Yuga* into a *Kali Yuga*. Most references to Kali Yuga term it as the final stage – often represented as a dystopian age of darkness, ignorance and destruction of the dharmic order.

4 Koestler, A. (1967). *The Ghost in the Machine*. London: Hutchinson.

5 Lewin, K. (1936). *Principles of Topological Psychology*. Read Books Limited.

6 The literal meaning of *Sutradhara* is "thread-holder". He is analogous to a modern director, stage manager and producer. The etymology suggests that he holds the metaphorical thread and holds together the various incidents in a play. In any play, he could not only impersonate a character but also voice aloud characters' inner thoughts or feelings whenever those were not revealed explicitly. He often intervenes between scenes with meta-theatrical remarks about his actors or the action. At the end, he appears again to deliver the closing stanza of the text. Thus, he holds the center of activities while keeping his presence in the background. The Sutradhar plays many roles including the director, narrator, singer, reciter or commentator in theatrical forms all over India.

Chapter 4

Findings from EUM data

In this chapter, we offer our analysis of data collected through the deployment of the EUM-I and EUM-O instruments, in more than 100 organizations and over 5,000 individuals.

Since our basic purpose is to explore the impact of Indian psyche on the corporate world, we have pruned our database to only such respondents who can be clearly identified as INDIANS and clearly belong to the world of CORPORATES. All such cases where the demographics were not clear and where there was an ambiguity on either of the two factors were eliminated. It still leaves us with a reasonably substantial database of *more than* 4,000 respondents.

Some of the interesting features of our findings include the following:

1   There have been no significant changes in findings over last 20 years that EUM has been in existence.
2   The results resonate strongly with the findings of the research on work values of Indian managers conducted way back in 1974.
3   There are no significant differences across demographic cuts of gender, age and types of organizations.

Keeping the preceding in mind, it would appear that these findings are indicative of civilizational predispositions of Indians (in the corporate world) cutting across differences of age, gender, generational groups and types of organization. However, to what extent they also apply to other socioeconomic groups is a matter of conjecture.

Part I

Analysis of EUM-I data

Annexure 4.1 gives the average ranks for the 15 adjectives and the mean scores for the six Universes for the three dimensions, that is, SC or 'I am', SI or 'I aspire to be' and OP or 'my perception of other people'. It also gives the overall difference between SC, SI and OP. Annexure 4.2 gives the correlations between the Universe scores.

The way the instrument is designed, 150 points are distributed across the six Universes with the proviso that no individual Universe can have a score of more than 50. Thus, the scores have both an absolute value (on a scale of 0 to 50) and a proportionate value.

For example, a score of 30 will mean 60% in an absolute sense (30 out of a maximum of 50) and a proportionate value of 20% (i.e., higher than the expected value of 16.67% if all Universes were equally represented).

Table 4.1 summarizes the Universe scores for EUM-I for all the respondents across the three categories.

The following themes can be discerned from this data.

Table 4.1 Universe scores- EUM-I

Universes	Mean		
	SC (I am)	SI (I aspire to be)	OP (My perception of other people)
Belonging & Protection (UBP)	22.18	19.81	23.31
Strength & Desire (USD)	**18.71**	19.08	27.62
Roles & Boundaries (URB)	**30.82**	29.14	25.86
Purpose & Achievement (UPA)	30.38	**35.87**	**32.69**
Meaningfulness & Intimacy (UMI)	22.80	**17.23**	**17.95**
Duality & Simultaneity (UDS)	25.10	28.87	22.80

Note: The highest and lowest scores in each column have been given in boldface.

Theme I

THE INDIAN MANAGER AND THE PROCESSES OF IDENTIFICATION

Table 4.1 shows that the Universe most *identified* with by our respondents is URB with an SC ("I am") score of 30.82.

While UPA scores for SC (30.38) are also quite high and only marginally lower than URB (SC = 30.82), there is considerable difference in what these two Universes signify to our respondents.

In case of URB the OP score (25.86) is significantly lower than SC (30.82), but in case of UPA the OP (32.69) score is higher.

This difference suggests that the Indian manager is telling him- or herself that while he or she may identify with both these Universes in equal measure, in comparison to other people, the manager finds him- or herself a lot more in URB and a little less in UPA. The difference becomes even more significant when we see that while the UPA scores go up from SC to SI, the URB scores come down.

Clearly in a relative sense, the identification with URB is much higher than with UPA. It may be noted that even in the research on values of Indian managers conducted way back in 1974, the Conformistic level (equivalent of URB) had emerged as the most significant one. Thus, it would seem that these scores are indicative of a civilizational preference for role appropriateness and structural clarity. Furthermore, the drop from SC to SI in URB scores suggests some unease with this predisposition.

What our respondents seem to be saying is that perhaps they are a bit too concerned with role and structure and thus are not able to give sufficient elbow room to themselves to pursue their UPA orientation to the extent that they would like to.

This feeling of being shackled is perhaps getting accentuated by the fact that the Universe our respondents **least identify** with is USD. The SC score of **18.71** is the lowest among all Universes and is substantially lower than OP (27.62). Thus, USD is identified with neither in an absolute sense nor in a relative sense. Since the USD scores also remain low in SI, the Universe is also not valued much. Here again we find that in the 1974 research, Egocentric level (equivalent of USD) was the lowest.

Our hypothesis is that this aversion towards USD is dealt with by projecting it on to other people.

Overall, what is indicated by these data is the following:

• Indian managers have a great need for role clarity and structural sanctity.
• They find it difficult to acknowledge their own needs and desires and have a propensity to project them on to others.
• They lay greater emphasis on role performance than the pursuit of ambition.
• They experience difficulties in engaging with *aggression*, both within oneself and others.

Theme 2

THE INDIAN MANAGER ON 'HOW DO I DEFINE MYSELF?'

The UBP scores for SC (22.18) for our respondents are higher than SC scores for USD (18.71), which suggests that the belonging system is a stronger anchor of identity for them rather than their personal distinctiveness.

In the EUM framework, UBP and USD are regarded as the main building blocks of Identity. A leaning towards UBP indicates a more "relational orientation" whereas a leaning towards USD indicates an individualistic orientation. Thus, the Indian managers are likely to derive their sense of 'Self' from the system/group/clan/organization to which they belong.

Simply put, they seem to be saying, "*I am defined more by where I come from and where I belong rather than by my personal attributes*" – and thus, the need to belong becomes a powerful source of one's identity.

This is likely to get manifested in the following:

1 There is a need to forge affiliative links.
2 There is a strong sense of commitment/loyalty to the belonging system (work group, department, organization, etc.).
3 There is a high concern with how one is seen by one's reference group.
4 There is preoccupation with processes of inclusion and exclusion.
5 Engagement with others for the Indian manager is impacted by "where the person comes from" rather than "what he or she brings to the table".

Theme 3

COMPETITIVENESS AND SIBLING RIVALRY

The USD scores for the Indian managers provide an insight on how he or she encounters, engages and processes feelings of competitiveness and envy – two feelings that are unique to this Universe. Our analysis reveals that these two feelings are very difficult for the Indian manager to express and engage with, and hence, there is a complex process by which these feelings are worked through.

If we look at the scores of our respondents in Table 4.2, where we compare scores of USD and UBP, USD scores for both SC (18.71) and SI (19.08) are much lower than OP scores (27.62).

What our respondents seem to be saying is "*The world at large is USD driven, but I am not, nor do I wish to*". Thus, many of the inherent feelings intrinsic to USD such as competitiveness and envy belong to the Other and not me!

The scores of Belonging and Protection perhaps reveal how the Indian manager copes with the denial of USD within Self, including taboo feelings that are salient to it. We believe that the Indian manager finds it easier to work with competitiveness and envy by preferring to looking at any system as a clan or a family as opposed to an arena or a battlefield. As a result, competitiveness is seen as legitimate only in relation to those who are outside the clan/family. In the internal dynamics, competitiveness gets translated into sibling rivalry.

Some of the implications are as follows:

1   There is a clear bifurcation between competitors (outsiders) and collaborators (insiders).

Table 4.2 UBP and USD scores

Universes	Mean		
	SC (I am)	SI (I aspire to be)	OP (my perception of other people)
Belonging & Protection (UBP)	22.18	19.81	23.31
Strength & Desire (USD)	**18.71**	19.08	**27.62**

2 Differential rewards are more likely to be seen as "bestowals" from an authority (parent) figure rather than having being earned by the individual through own merits.

3 The individual is likely to look up to a 'father' or 'mother' figure to ensure an equitable treatment.

4 Setbacks in competitive situations are likely to be experienced as acts of unfair discrimination.

Theme 4

THE INDIAN MANAGER ON HUMANENESS AND SELF-RIGHTEOUSNESS: *THE SPLIT WITHIN!*

In Table 4.3, which compares the scores of URB and UMI, we find that the scores for Others are much lower than SC.

Simultaneously, the scores for USD are much higher in OP than SC. This is an interesting split between Self and Others within which the Indian manager seems to operate.

The implicit statement here being that "*I am more driven by humanistic considerations, norms and structural discipline than most other people*". This perhaps becomes a self-righteous stance for the Indian manager, thus making it very difficult to work with his or her disowned Strength and Desired scores.

The same phenomenon can be witnessed in the relative ranks of different adjectives in SC and OP.

Table 4.4 reveals that the top-ranking adjectives for SC (I am) are *Rational, Fair, Collaborative* and *Dutiful* (in bold).

The top-ranking adjectives in Others (again appearing in bold) are *Competitive, Tactful, Cautious*, and Tough Also, *in all four, OP* ranks are much higher than SC.

Table 4.3 URB and UMI scores

Universes	Mean		
	SC (I am)	SI (I aspire to be)	OP (perceptions of others)
Roles & Boundaries (URB)	30.82	29.14	**25.86**
Meaningfulness & Intimacy (UMI)	22.80	17.23	**17.95**

Table 4.4 Adjectives ranking – EUM-I

Adjectives	SC	SI	OP (perceptions of others)
Rational	**5.21**	5.30	7.02
Sacrificing	10.47	12.26	12.85
Gracious	8.80	8.32	9.07
Cautious	9.09	10.43	**6.63**
Emotional	8.92	11.81	8.77
Competitive	7.45	6.38	**5.23**
Sympathetic	8.32	9.66	9.26
Uninhibited	11.18	9.55	9.82
Collaborative	**5.69**	5.72	7.09
Dutiful	**5.70**	7.18	7.82
Fair	**5.29**	5.95	8.11
Tactful	9.60	7.67	**5.96**
Tough	9.65	7.81	**6.94**
Dynamic	6.66	4.46	7.00
Steady	7.96	8.00	8.43

Note: The top four ranks in SC and OP are in boldface.

Put together, these different pieces make a fairly cogent picture. What the typical Indian manager (as represented in our sample) seems to be saying is something like

> *I am part of a system and like to respect its norms. I try to fulfill my role obligations and strive to achieve my goals within the boundaries laid down by the system without violating humanistic values. However, I am in a context where there is less respect for either systemic discipline or humanistic considerations.*

Thus, the picture of the Self is of a simple amiable and honest person who wishes to live with honor and dignity. In contrast, the "OTHER" is seen as a closed, self-absorbed person who primarily relies on connivance to get along or get ahead in life.

A significant implication of this splitting is that there is likely to be a wide gap between the outward behavior of the individual from what he or she actually thinks or feels. This gap can become both a source of strength as also cause difficulties. On one hand, it enables the individual to demonstrate high levels of resilience and behavioral flexibility to deal with adversity, but on the other hand, it can make the person appear as inconsistent and unreliable.

Theme 5

THE TENSION BETWEEN UPA AND UMI – HOW DOES THE INDIAN
MANAGER CO-HOLD THESE WITHIN?

Table 4.5 that shows the scores for UPA and UMI, reveals that the
sharpest increase from SC (30.38) to SI (35.87) across the six Universes is in UPA.

This is perhaps reflective of the predominance of UPA/Network
culture in the present-day world, particularly in the corporate sector representing market capitalism.

Simultaneously the sharpest drop from SC (22.80) to SI (17.23)
across the six Universes is in UMI.

This suggests that these two Universes have a contra-pull in the
minds of our respondents. This contra-pull gets reinforced by the
correlations between the six Universes scores for EUM-I for SC
shown in Table 4.6.

As can be seen from the above table, the highest negative correlation is between the Universes of UPA and UMI (–0.54). While the
structure of the instrument is such that there is an inbuilt negative

Table 4.5 UPA and UMI scores

Universes	Mean		
	SC (I am)	SI (I aspire to be)	OP (perceptions of others)
Purpose & Achievement (UPA)	30.38	35.87	32.69
Meaningfulness & Intimacy (UMI)	22.80	17.23	17.95

Table 4.6 SC: correlations

	UBP	USD	URB	UPA	UMI	UDS
UBP	1.00	−0.29	−0.10	−0.20	−0.18	−0.30
USD	−0.29	1.00	−0.21	−0.07	−0.15	−0.19
URB	−0.10	−0.21	1.00	−0.26	−0.11	−0.11
UPA	−0.20	−0.07	−0.26	1.00	**−0.54**	0.06
UMI	−0.18	−0.15	−0.11	**−0.54**	1.00	−0.27
UDS	−0.30	−0.19	−0.11	0.06	−0.27	1.00

correlation between all Universes, in the case of UPA and UMI, it is much more than others.

Simply put, what our respondents seem to be saying is *"If I wish to enhance my UPA orientation then I must reduce my UMI orientation"*.

This suggests that the Indian managers are experiencing considerable tension between demands of "meritocracy" and "humanistic values". This could well be because being humanistic gets interpreted more in the sense of being nice, soft and polite rather than in the sense of being open and authentic.

If this is so, then chances are that they are likely to focus more on "interface management" than "authentic encounter".

There is some support for this hypothesis from the fact that UBP scores do not fall as sharply as UMI from SC to SI.

Theme 6

SIGNIFICANCE OF SMOOTH RELATIONSHIPS

One of the patterns that stands out is the Indian manager looking at the notion of SI and the key shifts that he or she wishes to make in order to be seen as effective, ambitious and successful.

We discovered that, as shown in Table 4.7, which depicts the SI correlations, the negative correlation between UPA and UBP is very negligible (–0.071) whereas it is quite high between UPA and UMI (–0.451).

This is counterintuitive to the notion of UPA, where the individual sees him- or herself as the 'self-centered, meritocratic, competent, challenging legacies and interdependent' person, shunning any notions of dependency, loyalty or clannishness as offered by UBP.

Apparently, the Indian manager feels that in order to be effective, it is more important to have smooth and harmonious relationships

Table 4.7 SI: correlations

	UBP	USD	URB	UPA	UMI	UDS
UBP	1.00	–0.26	–0.14	–0.07	–0.35	–0.26
USD	–0.26	1.00	–0.27	–0.04	–0.20	–0.19
URB	–0.14	–0.27	1.00	–0.26	–0.06	–0.15
UPA	–0.07	–0.04	–0.26	1.00	–0.45	–0.17
UMI	–0.35	–0.20	–0.06	–0.45	1.00	–0.09
UDS	–0.26	–0.19	–0.15	–0.17	–0.09	1.00

than upholding human values like inclusivity, transparency, authenticity and the like.

Not surprisingly if we were to look at adjectives ranking again, shown in Table 4.8, we find that the adjectives that increased in rank from SC to SI are *Dynamic*, *Competitive*, *Tactful*, *Tough* and *Uninhibited*.

Table 4.8 Adjectives ranking and desired shifts – EUM-1

Adjectives	SC	SI	Desired Shift
Rational	5.21	5.30	–
Sacrificing	10.47	12.26	↓
Gracious	8.80	8.32	
Cautious	9.09	10.43	↓
Emotional	8.92	11.81	↓
Competitive	7.48	6.38	↑
Sympathetic	8.32	9.66	↓
Uninhibited	11.18	9.55	↑
Collaborative	5.69	5.72	
Dutiful	5.70	7.18	↓
Fair	5.29	5.95	
Tactful	9.60	7.37	↑
Tough	9.65	7.76	↑
Dynamic	6.66	4.36	↑
Steady	7.96	7.94	

On the other hand, the adjectives that decrease in rank from SC to SI are *Emotional, Dutiful, Sacrificing, Sympathetic* and *Cautious*. Our speculation is that through these shifts, the Indian managers are expressing two *wishes*:

1 To find greater freedom and mobility for themselves through greater dynamism and spontaneity
2 To enhance interpersonal effectiveness through becoming more tactful and tough

We believe what links these two wishes is the connection between "self-authorization" and "smooth interfaces" for the Indian manager. When the individual finds him- or herself in a network of smooth relationships, the individual can give more freedom to him- or herself to become spontaneous and dynamic.

Part 2

Analysis of EUM-O data

Annexure 4.3 gives the average ranks for the 20 adjectives as also the mean scores for the six Universes, for the three dimensions of OC, or 'how I see my organization', OI or 'my picture of an Ideal organization' and MOO or 'my perception of most other organizations'. It also gives the overall differences between OC, OI and MOO.

The way the instrument is designed, 300 points are distributed across six Universes with the proviso that no single Universe can have more than 100 points. Thus, just as in case of EUM-I, the scores have an absolute value and a proportional value.

The EUM-O enables us to construct the picture in the mind of how the Indian manager looks at OC, OI and MOO. Let us begin with the average Universe scores as summarized in Table 4.9.

The main highlights that enable us to build a picture of the mind of the Indian manager are as follows:

1 *My organization is more clannish and less of an Arena as compared to other organizations*
   The CLAN scores are slightly higher for OC as compared to MOO (43.88 > 41.44), whereas the ARENA scores are higher for MOO as compared to OC (49.43 > 46.94).

Table 4.9 Universe rank scores for EUM-O

Universes	Mean		
	OC	OI	MOO
Clan	43.88	33.00	41.44
Arena	46.94	39.39	49.43
Clockwork	51.99	51.23	53.85
Network	52.42	55.92	59.02
Ecology	47.09	41.93	33.91
Holonic	57.68	78.53	62.34

The OI scores for both Clan and Arena are significantly lower than for both OC and MOO. Thus, our respondents are not very happy with either the clannish nature of their own organizations or with the preponderance of Arena in other organizations.

2 *My organization is more Humanistic and Inclusive as opposed to other organizations, though we lose out on meritocracy, ambition and achievement.*

The Ecological scores are significantly higher for OC (47.09) as compared to MOO (33.91), whereas the Network scores are higher in MOO (59.02) as compared to OC (52.42).

In both cases, the OI scores fall somewhere between the OC and MOO scores. This implies that our respondents want their organization to enhance the Network orientation but not as much as other organizations. Similarly, they want their organization to be a little less humanistic but not go as low as other organizations.

3 *For my organization to evolve further, we need to lower our Clan, Arena, and Ecological mind-set.*

Looking at what needs to be changed (the difference between OI and OC), the Indian manager wishes to see the sharpest jump in the sixth Universe – Holonic registers the sharpest jump from 57.68 to 78.53, whereas there is a marginal increase in Network Universe. Correspondingly the Indian manager wishes to see the Clan, Ecological and Arena show significant drops from OC to OI.

Table 4.10 gives the average ranks for the various adjective and the shifts that our respondents on EUM-O would like to see in them.

4 *I can hold the ethicality of my organization with pride – the other specifics of my organization do not really matter or are held with negative tonality.*
   If we look at the Table 4.10, the adjectives that register the sharpest upward jump from OC to OI are *Strategic, Efficient, Creative, Empowering, Decisive* and *Disciplined*. Simultaneously, the adjectives that register the sharpest fall from OC to OI are *Hierarchical, Diplomatic, Personalized, Informal* and *Demanding*.

   It is important to distinguish some of the shifts mentioned earlier as seen by our respondents as 'GENERIC' (applicable to all organizations) from other shifts which are seen as 'SPECIFIC' (applicable particularly to their own organizations). We look at organizations being generic if the difference between OC and MOO is not very high.

Table 4.10 EUM-O mean scores for adjectives

Adjectives	Mean			Desired shift	Generic/ Specific
	OC	OI	MOO	OC-OI	
Flexible	7.93	8.13	9.12	−0.20	
Collaborative	8.94	7.33	8.50	1.65	Generic
Efficient	9.32	5.72	7.01	3.60	Specific
Hierarchical	9.71	15.18	8.40	−5.47	Generic
Benevolent	11.59	13.25	13.39	−1.66	
Strategic	8.66	4.65	5.70	4.01	Specific
Ethical	6.30	6.10	10.38	0.20	
Informal	10.78	13.27	12.95	−2.49	Specific
Caring	10.38	10.63	12.73	−0.25	
Diligent	10.74	11.49	11.10	−0.75	
Empowering	9.87	7.12	10.23	2.75	Generic
Personalized	11.98	15.52	13.88	−3.54	Specific
Decisive	12.20	8.79	9.16	3.41	Specific
Creative	12.22	8.05	10.79	4.17	Generic
Expedient	13.33	13.98	12.54	−0.65	
Demanding	9.76	11.71	8.36	−1.95	
Diplomatic	12.62	16.09	12.63	−3.47	Generic
Ambitious	8.56	7.73	6.98	−0.83	Specific
Protective	13.23	15.71	15.61	−2.48	Specific
Disciplined	11.88	9.56	10.55	2.32	Specific

For example, all organizations are GENERICALLY seen as *overly hierarchical* and *overly diplomatic*. Similarly, not being sufficiently *empowering* and creative is seen as a feature that is common to all organizations.

On the other hand, being *less* strategic/efficient/decisive/disciplined and being over personalized/informal are seen by our respondents as specific issues of their own organizations.

The only adjective for which the OI rank is significantly closer to OC than MOO is *Ethical*. This suggests that the primary source of pride that our respondents have with respect to their organizations comes from their belief that it is more ethical than other organizations.

To a lesser extent, they also seem to have some good feeling that their organization is a bit more flexible, a bit more caring and a bit less demanding.

In most other spheres, they seem to believe that other organizations are better than their organization; for example, they are more strategic, more efficient, more decisive and more disciplined.

5   One of the essential differences that our respondents see between their organization and other organizations is with respect to ambition. The MOO rank for *Ambitious* is significantly higher than OC. Interestingly, the OI rank falls right in the center. What this suggests is that our respondents want their own organization to become more "ambitious" but not "as ambitious as other organizations".

6   Coupled with the rest of the data, our hypothesis is that "*in the minds of our respondents their own organization is held as relatively safer but not very exciting. The external world is seen as both inviting and adventurous, on one hand, and unkind and dangerous, on the other. While they do not quite like the clannish and overly humanistic orientation of their own organization, they are equally uncomfortable with the high Arena and low Humanistic orientation of other organizations*".

Part 3

Putting the two together: EUM-I and EUM-O

There are many commonalities as also complementarities between the EUM-I and EUM-O data. Table 4.11 becomes the basis of putting our findings from EUM-I and EUM-O together.

Table 4.11 Comparison of Universe scores between EUM-I and EUM-O

EUM-I	Mean			EUM-O	Mean		
	SC	SI	Others		OC	OI	MOO
UBP	22.18	19.81	23.31	**Clan**	43.88	33.00	41.44
USD	18.71	19.08	27.62	**Arena**	46.94	39.39	49.43
URB	30.82	29.14	25.86	**Clockwork**	51.99	51.23	53.85
UPA	30.38	35.87	32.69	**Network**	52.42	55.92	59.02
UMI	22.80	17.23	17.95	**Ecology**	47.09	41.93	33.91
UDS	25.10	28.87	22.57	**Holonic**	57.68	78.53	62.34

Some of the themes that emerge follow.

Theme 1

STRONG IDENTIFICATION WITH THE ORGANIZATION

There is considerable overlap between the perception of our respondents about themselves and their organizations. In both cases, the three top-ranked and bottom-ranked Universes are the same, though there is some difference in their relative position. In case of Self, the top three are URB, UPA and UDS, whereas in case of the organization, they are Holonic (UDS), Network (UPA) and Clockwork (URB). Similarly, the bottom three for the Self are UMI, UBP and USD, whereas in case of the organization they are Ecology (UMI), Arena (USD) and Clan (UBP).

In both cases, Holonic (UDS) and Network (UPA) go up in SI and OI, and Ecology (UMI), Clockwork (URB) and Clan (UBP) come down.

Thus, it appears that our respondents have a high degree of identification with their organizations; that is, they see themselves and their organizations as quite similar.

Theme 2

TENSION BETWEEN HUMANISTIC VALUES AND
ACHIEVEMENT ORIENTATION

The identicality between Self and organization is most stark in respect of UMI and Ecological, on one hand, and UPA and

Network, on the other. In both UMI and Ecological, the scores given to the self-SC and OC are much greater than the scores given to the other – OP and MOO, respectively.

Furthermore, in both cases, there is significant drop from the current state (SC and OC) to the ideal state (SI and OI, respectively) Simultaneously, the UPA and Network scores are seen as slightly higher in the other (OP and MOO, respectively) than in the Self (SC and OC, respectively).

Thus, whether it be at the level of the individual or at the level of the collective/system, the position of our respondents remains essentially the same.

Broadly what the Indian manager seems to be saying is

> The world at large is self-seeking and does not care much about human values. My/our greater humanistic orientation is a liability and comes in the way of pursuing meritocracy. I/we will be better off by curtailing some of my/our humanistic orientation.

Perhaps, this belief/position is part of the same process of splitting referred to earlier. In other words, holding onto the picture of a "self-seeking, insensitive, non-caring" world enables our respondents to look at themselves as "well-meaning, innocent victims" who are forced to become like "others" in order to cope and survive in this harsh and "dog-eat-dog" world.

To what extent, this belief/position becomes a self-fulfilling prophecy is worth exploring.

Theme 3

FEELING LET DOWN BY THE SYSTEM

Looking at the Table 4.12, we find that in EUM-I, the gap between SC and SI (44.80) is much smaller than the gap between OC and OI (100.25), in case of EUM-O.

Table 4.12 Differences in EUM-I and EUM-O

EUM-I Differences		EUM-O Differences	
SC–SI	44.80	OC–OI	100.25
SI–OP	57.09	OI–MOO	88.64
SC–OP	64.92	OC–MOO	113.02

Similarly, in EUM-I, SI is much closer to SC than OP [(SC–SI) = 44.80 < (SI–OP]) = 57.09)), but the reverse is the case for EUM-O, where OI is closer to MOO than OC (OI–OC < OI–MOO or 100.25 > 88.64).

In other words, what our respondents seem to be saying, "I am okay as compared to Self Ideal, and systemic deficiencies in my organization form the root cause of my difficulty".

This suggests that our respondents have a feeling of being let down by the system and perhaps an expectation that the system will be more responsive to their struggles and difficulties. This disappointment can also lead to a situation, where the individual manager can take the role of an outsider/commentator/helpless victim and disown responsibility both for the self and for the system.

Theme 4

AMBIVALENCE TOWARDS AMBITION/COMPETITIVENESS

Looking at the Table 4.13, we find an interesting complementarity in the adjective analysis – in case of EUM-O, we find that *Ambitious* in OI falls right in the center of OC and MOO.

Similarly, in EUM-I, we find *Competitive* in SI to be right in the center of SC and OP.

Our hypothesis is that the difficulty in acknowledging one's own needs and the hesitation to assert directly are experienced both at the self level as well as at the system level and is held in ambivalence.

Simultaneously, our respondents feel the need to be more competitive/ambitious but are unable to grace it and embrace it wholeheartedly. This could perhaps be due to the fact that becoming more competitive/ambitious is seen as a necessary requirement to survive and grow in the present-day world rather than as an intrinsic evocation.

Table 4.13 Adjective analysis EUM-I and EUM-O

EUM-I	SC	SI	Others
Competitive	7.45	6.38	5.23
EUM-O	**OC**	**OI**	**MOO**
Ambitious	8.56	7.73	6.98

Theme 5

SEARCH FOR A "PERFECT SYSTEM"

We had mentioned earlier about the high identification of the Indian managers with their organizations.

Simultaneously, they seem to be carrying some feelings of being let down by their organizations. We suspect, that these get translated into a search for a perfect system.

Thus, in some cases, we find that the direction of change being sought for the system (the organization) is contrary to the change being sought for Self, as shown in the Table 4.14.

The starkest example of this is the comparison on *Diplomatic* (an adjective used in EUM-O) and *Tactful* (an adjective used in EUM-I).

Whereas *Diplomatic* registers a sharp fall from OC to OI in EUM-O, *Tactful*, on the other hand, registers a rise from SC to SI in case of EUM-I.

In other words, what our respondents seem to be saying is "*The system needs to become more straightforward (less diplomatic) but I need to become less so (more tactful)*".

The case with *Demanding* (an adjective used in EUM-O) and *Tough* (an adjective used in EUM-I) is similar, wherein our respondents want to become tougher but want the system to become less demanding.

Our hypothesis is that *through these seemingly conflicting wishes, our respondents are perhaps seeking a "perfect system" that does not require them to take any interpersonal risk.*

In other words, our respondents seem to recognize the need to assert more directly. However, given the significance, which they attach to smooth interfaces, they wish that the system would become more straightforward (less diplomatic) and less demanding, which, in turn, would enable them to assert more directly without

Table 4.14 Comparison of desired shifts between EUM-I and EUM-O

EUM-I	SC	SI	Shift desired	EUM-O	OC	OI	Shift desired
Tactful	9.60	7.37	⬆	**Diplomatic**	12.62	16.09	⬇
Tough	9.65	7.76	⬆	**Demanding**	9.76	11.71	⬇

upsetting the matrix of their relationships. In absence of this situation, they feel the need to become tougher and more tactful in order
to cope with the imperfections of the system.

Theme 6

EMPOWERMENT WITHOUT SELF-AUTHORIZATION

Per Table 4.15, the adjective which registers the sharpest fall from
OC to OI (from 9.71 to 15.18) is *Hierarchical.*

Simultaneously, the adjective *Empowering* moves up from OC
to OI. This is perhaps indicative of the high-power distance and
hierarchical orientation in Indian culture.

However, what the EUM-I data suggest is that this desired shift
may be as much an issue of personal propensity of the individual
Indian manager as that of systemic features of the organization he
or she works in.

Given that in the Indian psyche, USD is neither identified with
nor valued enough, it is perhaps not very easy for our respondents
to empower or authorize themselves, and consequently, the experience of "hierarchical oppression" is at least partly self-created.

It is therefore likely that they expect that the system will somehow release them from this oppression and thereby help them to
feel "empowered", without them having to invest into the USD.

Table 4.15 Comparison of desired shifts between EUM-I and EUM-O

EUM-I	SC	SI	Shift	EUM-O	OC	OI	Shift
USD	18.71	19.08	–	Hierarchical	9.71	15.18	⬇
URB	30.82	29.14	–	Empowering	9.87	7.12	⬆

Theme 7

NEED FOR STRUCTURAL LEGITIMACY TO EXERCISE CONTROL

An interesting feature of data from EUM-I is the orientation of our
respondents towards Control. The significantly higher SC score in

URB as compared to OP suggests a high need for control. This is accounted for by the individual's belief that most people do not pay as much attention to systemic discipline as necessary.

However, the USD scores are much lower in SC than in OP. The implication of this is that other people are likely to be seen as more aggressive and, hence, more difficult to control.

Given this scenario, our hypothesis is that *Indian managers need a high degree of systemic provisions and legitimacy to exercise control. In structurally ambiguous situations (e.g., complex matrix or informal networked structures) they may find it difficult to empower themselves and exercise control to the extent that they would like to.*

It is therefore not surprising that both *Decisive* and *Disciplined* go up appreciably from OC to OI in EUM-O data.

Table 4.16 Comparison of desired shifts between EUM-I and EUM-O

EUM-I	SC	SI	Others	EUM-O	OC	OI	Shift
USD	18.71	19.08	27.62	Disciplined	11.88	9.56	Increase
URB	30.82	29.14	25.86	Decisive	12.2	8.79	Increase

Theme 8

TENSION BETWEEN STRUCTURAL SANCTITY AND
PERSONAL AFFILIATION

A similar transference of a personal difficulty to a systemic expectation, as seen in the earlier point, is evidenced in the sharp drop from OC to OI with respect to the adjective *Personalized*.

Given a high URB orientation and relatively high UBP orientation, it is highly likely that our respondents experience considerable conflict between affiliation and role sanctity.

Table 4.17 Comparison of desired shifts between EUM-I and EUM-O.

EUM-I	SC	SI	Others	EUM-O	OC	OI	Shift
UBP	22.18	19.81	23.31	Personalized	11.98	15.52	Less of
URB	30.82	29.14	25.86				

Their UBP orientation is likely to make them seek the comfort of close and personalized relationships. However, the high URB orientation will push them towards role-based, depersonalized relationships.

Our hypothesis is that through *"wishing the system to become less personalized, perhaps our respondents are shifting this conflict on to the system and hoping that it will settle it for them"*.

Summing up

The broad picture that emerges from the analysis of our data about Indian managers and their relatedness with the organization is as follows:

1 They tend to define themselves more in relational terms than in individualistic terms.
2 They believe that most other people and organizations are governed by "self-interest" and hence not very dependable/trustworthy.
3 They wish to embrace their aspirations but remain ambivalent about their needs and desires. Hence, they would need the justification/legitimacy of "systemic needs" to own up to their own ambitions.
4 They believe that maintaining harmonious relationships is critical to their success and effectiveness. Broader humanistic values, such as inclusivity, transparency and authenticity, seem relatively less important to them.
5 They are likely to feel energized in a context that provides a high degree of belonging and provides sufficient elbow room and space for expression.
6 They need considerable role clarity and structural legitimacy.
7 They are likely to experience some conflict between personalized relationships and sanctity of roles.
8 They are likely to deal with conflict through adjustment, compromise and indirect/subtle ways and tend to avoid direct confrontation.
9 They prefer to blend continuity with change rather than make radical departures.
10 They feel suffocated by high hierarchical orientation in the context but find it difficult to empower themselves.

11 They are likely to be good at sensing the power dynamics in any situation and adapt themselves accordingly. Also, they are likely to juggle their way through conflicting demands from multiple power centers.

12 They are likely to attribute their difficulties to systemic limitation and, hence, carry a feeling of being "let down" by the system.

13 They are likely to demonstrate a high degree of resilience and behavioral flexibility in dealing with adversity.

14 They are likely to seek strong emotive links and would find it easier to empower themselves when they feel secure in the network of relationships around themselves.

EUM-I mean adjective ranks and scores for the Universes
N = 4211

	SC	SI	Others
Rational	5.21	5.30	7.02
Sacrificing	10.47	12.26	12.85
Gracious	8.80	8.32	9.07
Cautious	9.09	10.43	6.63
Emotional	8.92	11.81	8.77
Competitive	7.45	6.38	5.23
Sympathetic	8.32	9.66	9.26
Uninhibited	11.18	9.55	9.82
Collaborative	5.69	5.72	7.09
Dutiful	5.70	7.18	7.82
Fair	5.29	5.95	8.11
Tactful	9.60	7.38	5.96
Tough	9.65	7.76	6.94
Dynamic	6.66	4.36	7.00
Steady	7.96	7.94	8.43

Universe			
	SC	SI	Others
Belongingness & Protection	22.18	19.81	23.31
Strengths & Desires	18.71	19.08	27.62
Roles & Boundaries	30.82	29.14	25.86
Purpose & Achievement	30.38	35.87	32.69
Meaningfulness & Intimacy	22.80	17.23	17.95
Duality & Simultaneity	25.10	28.87	22.57

Differences	
SC–SI	44.80
SI–OP	57.09
SC–OP	64.92

Appendix 4.2

EUM-I correlation between Universes

	Self-Concept					
	B&P	S&D	R&B	P&A	M&I	D&S
B&P	1.00	−0.29	−0.10	−0.20	−0.18	−0.30
S&D	−0.29	1.00	−0.21	−0.07	−0.15	−0.19
R&B	−0.10	−0.21	1.00	−0.26	−0.11	−0.11
P&A	−0.20	−0.07	−0.26	1.00	−0.54	0.06
M&I	−0.18	−0.15	−0.11	−0.54	1.00	−0.27
D&S	−0.30	−0.19	−0.11	0.06	−0.27	1.00

	Self-Ideal					
	B&P	S&D	R&B	P&A	M&I	D&S
B&P	1.00	−0.26	−0.14	−0.07	−0.35	−0.26
S&D	−0.26	1.00	−0.27	−0.04	−0.20	−0.19
R&B	−0.14	−0.27	1.00	−0.26	−0.06	−0.15
P&A	−0.07	−0.04	−0.26	1.00	−0.45	−0.17
M&I	−0.35	−0.20	−0.06	−0.45	1.00	−0.09
D&S	−0.26	−0.19	−0.15	−0.17	−0.09	1.00

	Others					
	B&P	S&D	R&B	P&A	M&I	D&S
B&P	1.00	−0.11	−0.20	−0.13	−0.32	−0.27
S&D	−0.11	1.00	−0.40	−0.08	−0.21	−0.31
R&B	−0.20	−0.40	1.00	−0.19	0.00	−0.03
P&A	−0.13	−0.08	−0.19	1.00	−0.51	−0.04
M&I	−0.32	−0.21	0.00	−0.51	1.00	−0.15
D&S	−0.27	−0.31	−0.03	−0.04	−0.15	1.00

Note: B&P = Belonging and Protection; S&D = Strength & Desire; R&B = Roles & Boundaries; P&A = Purpose and Achievement; M&I = Meaningfulness and Intimacy; D&S = Duality and Simultaneity.

EUM-O: mean adjective ranks and scores for Universes

Adjectives	Mean		
	OC	OI	MOO
Flexible	7.93	8.13	9.12
Collaborative	8.94	7.33	8.50
Efficient	9.32	5.72	7.01
Hierarchical	9.71	15.18	8.40
Benevolent	11.59	13.25	13.39
Strategic	8.66	4.65	5.70
Ethical	6.30	6.10	10.38
Informal	10.78	13.27	12.95
Caring	10.38	10.63	12.73
Diligent	10.74	11.49	11.10
Empowering	9.87	7.12	10.23
Personalized	11.98	15.52	13.88
Decisive	12.20	8.79	9.16
Creative	12.22	8.05	10.79
Expedient	13.33	13.98	12.54
Demanding	9.76	11.71	8.36
Diplomatic	12.62	16.09	12.63
Ambitious	8.56	7.73	6.98
Protective	13.23	15.71	15.61
Disciplined	11.88	9.56	10.55

Universes	Mean		
	OC	OI	MOO
Clan	43.88	33.00	41.44
Arena	46.94	39.39	49.43
Clockwork	51.99	51.23	53.85
Network	52.42	55.92	59.02
Ecology	47.09	41.93	33.91
Holonic	57.68	78.53	62.34

Differences	
OC–OI	100.25
OI–MOO	88.64
OC–MOO	113.02

Chapter 5

An uneasy relationship

Part I

An illustrative case

The beginning . . .

Hema heard her iPhone X jingle away to let her know that it was time to leave for her first meeting with Ravi – one of her many direct reports and a factory head to boot. Hema had recently taken on the role of a business head (a mini CEO was what her boss termed it as) for a fairly large business with revenues crossing the thousand crores mark, with the objective of growing this business multifold.

As she instructed the maids on the household chores in a meticulous and detailed fashion, she thought about her impending meeting with Ravi. She had heard many things about this man from her global headquarters but was trying to keep her mind open and neutral.

She had started her career as a business consultant with one of the top three global consulting firms and then eight years quickly passed after she migrated to the East Coast in the US. A high ranker from an Ivy League business school and a chemical engineering graduate from an Indian Institute of Technology. Hema had a brilliant track record when it came to strategy and marketing. Naturally good with numbers, she exuded tremendous confidence and power as she engaged with assertive chief executive officers over strategic and change initiatives.

Marriage and then a daughter happened along the way, and both her husband and she were not too sure whether the US was the right country to bring up their daughter. Actually, her husband was quite clear that there was a need to come back to India and to

Bangalore, and she was reasonably open to the idea. Bangalore had good schools!

Moving back to India also meant giving herself the opportunity to manage a business from the inside and not as an external consultant. She felt that the eight years at the consulting firm had prepared her well with an all-around perspective of business. She wanted this opportunity as it would enable her to prove herself in the global business world.

A global pharmaceutical firm was the first to spot her and her credentials – she had worked with some of their leaders earlier, and in a matter of a couple of meetings, they offered her the role of a business head. They wanted her to stabilize and grow an existing business for a couple of years and promised her fairly attractive growth opportunities within their global leadership later.

The last eight weeks had blurred past her – she had moved countries, set up home in Bangalore, met up with the larger family that she had lost touch with and here she was planning to anchor the first ORM, or the operations review of the month, and meeting a diverse team that managed a huge plant in Mysuru area, a research and development center at Cuddalore (south of Chennai) and a huge team based in Bangalore.

The ORM was to happen the next day, but she wanted to meet Ravi first – the goals set by the global stakeholders were ambitious and she needed to know whether Ravi was up to it . . . the grapevine told her that he was not.

As her car rolled out of the gates of the society and on to the roads of Bangalore, choc-a-bloc with traffic, she sighed and picked up one of the folders titled Factory. Her HR head and her predecessor had compiled notes on the key people working in the factory, including Ravi. The factory had been set up in 1982 and had seen better days. Technology was brought in sporadically, but the main throughput system remained what it was – reasonably stable. In the last 18 months, the firm had set up three new lines in addition to the original line – there was sufficient space physically, but there was considerable resistance from Ravi and company.

Production planning was getting increasingly difficult as complex molecules were now brought under the ambit of the business – production was in smaller batches, requiring agility and flexibility. The quality team from the Bangalore office was panicking on a daily basis because batches were either not stable or did not meet standards.

Process consultants, quality experts and manufacturing gurus, among others, were coming every fortnight from everywhere – there were 10 parallel initiatives running at the plant – and each seemed to be oblivious of the other in terms of interdependency or impact.

The complaints from stakeholders were more or less the same – Ravi was seen as a closed manager, a bit of sphinx; data was never forthcoming easily; mistakes were rarely owned up; and he was constantly seen protecting his team of managers against the corporate teams. Her predecessor had written that the factory was like a fortress – one never knew the inside story. However, Ravi's team wrote glowing tributes about him each year. The Gallup survey continuously embellished his management style and leadership. The manufacturing head in the US was a big fan of Ravi's team.

Hema got out and walked briskly up to her office and found an older man with grayish hair waiting for her . . .

As Ravi waited at the business head's office for Hema, he found a comfortable chair and looked out at the enormous tree that peeked into the cabin. There was a squirrel that would move up and down the tree, oblivious of his interests, often ending up scratching the window pane.

While he looked calm and composed on the outside, he felt an odd twinge or two of anxiety inside – he had a new boss, and this one was a woman. He had never worked under a woman. He looked at any signs that would let him know about his new boss – the cabin looked quite impersonal except a small photograph of Hema and her daughter on some ski slopes.

There were many more books (that he had never read), however, on two newly constructed shelves, trophies and accreditations from universities (that he was not aware of) and souvenirs from various parts of the globe (that he never knew about) – the cabin looked 'classier', but he missed the beautiful Ganesha that occupied a whole corner.

On one side, a large whiteboard was neatly inscribed by financial and operational data – there were questions written in parallel to rows of data. A brand-new MacBook stared back from the recently polished table – and the cabin admittedly looked for lack of better words – "neater".

The company was changing, and Ravi was aware of it – the change was happening a bit too fast and in your face . . . as he looked back at his career.

Ravi had spent nearly 30 years with the firm. As a young graduate engineer trainee, he had been instrumental in setting up Line

1 – he had been well mentored by the managers that had come from the US. He was, in those days, seen as a good follower and a caring manager – a man who understood technology, operational rules, safety norms, compliance concerns and the need for control, given the nature of production.

Ravi was always seen as sincere, God-fearing, and committed, someone who could calmly and patiently manage any alarm or emergency – technical or personal – by just listening without reacting to begin with. Over the past three decades, he had invested his energies in knowing his team and even his workers. He looked at his team with great pride, just like a father would look at his sons.

Over the years, Ravi had handpicked his team under him – these were people who brought loyalty and great followership – people who were willing to learn from him. He was not very fond of high-fliers from famous engineering institutes or precocious city-bred kids – he had looked for people like himself – people who were interested in experiencing a career at this wonderful company – people who wanted to grow as the company grew.

He was not a braggart, but he knew that nobody could have enabled a commerce undergraduate dropout to not just complete his degree but to actually run a complex function of purchase as well. Some of his production staff were mere diploma holders[1] but, today, knew everything about Line 1 that could be known.

The team running the plant was one family – loyal and friendly – there were no disputes and no envy, at least not on the surface. If someone fell ill – the other would reach out and help. Ravi was known to have dinner meet every fortnight at his own place – families would come together and have fun. A lot more got done on such events – Ravi could invest in conversations with their wives and children – proffering advice or offering a shoulder to hear the small gripes . . .

His team and he had been effective in producing world class products . . . there was an occasional poor run . . . there was a rare untoward downtime . . . but they all worked hard to ensure that production targets were always met.

Ravi was also someone who understood tight budgetary control – his chief financial officer (CFO) was one of his ardent admirers in this process. Ravi intuitively understood what a deprivation mindset means – there were never any excesses as he ran a tight ship. New technology was cleverly scrutinized – cost control was a key goal. Ravi was skeptical of new fads and new-fangled information technology (IT) or ERP solutions.

Over the years, he was clear that he could manage operations and production – and that the company must trust and recognize his abilities in doing so. He had limited interaction with corporate headquarters apart from the quarterly meeting. He did not care much for people strolling into his plant and asking questions. His team was clearly instructed on the modus operandi of engaging with outsiders – they had to go through him.

It had taken him 30 years to reach thus far – he still had another six years to go. His children were in college, and his wife was currently shuttling between the factory and his village south of Madurai, where they were constructing a home.

Things had changed a lot in the last 18 months – the company had decided to expand from a one-line plant to having four complex lines. Much of the new technology and new products were complex and beyond his understanding. Suddenly the demands of the plant had grown manifold.

What had irritated him was that neither he nor his team had been included in the planning process – the senior vice president of manufacturing had largely consulted experts, as the Indian firm became the recipient of three lines that were earlier set up in South America. The design and engineering functions were run from the corporate, and he was just a spectator to seeing construction and commissioning happen on the adjacent land that had served as the cricket ground in the past . . .

Worse still, his boss had suddenly resigned, and the firm had chosen a woman from outside the world of pharmaceuticals to head the business. . .

He watched her come in . . . she seemed aggressive and purposive . . . and she had an American accent – a slight drawl that made her sound phony and began to steadily irritate him.

He had a simple plan – just get to know what is required of him and his team and negotiate these expectations hard – if these appeared unfair.

The rendezvous

Hema looked at Ravi – he appeared to be ordinary – there was a slight and perhaps false humility that he used with his superiors – a nasal tightening of his voice as his head would lean to one side, and his body would slump in the chair. Ravi had an old briefcase – from which he would occasionally and purposefully draw a file or two – his office had already sent her the Excel sheets structured on last year's budgets.

Ravi gazed expectantly for her to begin . . .

As she began speaking, she had an odd feeling of being scrutinized or being judged – her voice became harsher and drier as she spelled out the demands from the factory – these were tough demands not just in the form of outputs but also in terms of data sharing . . . She paused after some time as the slumped figure across from her seemed almost lifeless and passive.

"Well, what do you think . . . Mr. Ravikant?"

Ravi was surprised as Hema had offered only a perfunctory introduction of herself, and further disappointed that she did not delve into his background. Apparently, she had been briefed and had come with some prefixed notions. He blinked a couple of times and started talking about the unfair past – of his exclusion from the planning and commissioning project teams, of his exclusion from the initial interviews anchored by HR, of feeling let down as her predecessor had not anchored the transition well – there was no response from him on the goals and the expectations . . .

Hema felt her impatience climbing further as she pointed this out . . . He seemed to become more passive and restrained . . .

Hema was asking questions that he was not used to answering – some of these questions were about scenarios that he had no idea of. He was shocked that the teams transitioning the lines into India, had been circumspect of sharing data and details.

Quarterly targets were brought into the discussion, quite early by Hema, as he tried to brief her about the status of the plant. Did she really understand how a plant functions? Hema appeared to be impatient and overdemanding – he did not even have his team for Lines 2 through 4.

What struck him was that the whole meeting had been about numbers and not about people – Hema appeared disinterested in his intent to grow the team from within as opposed to hire from outside.

It also appeared that she was testing him, asking questions that he was not aware of and not offering her own solutions or ideas – what kind of a boss was he going to get? Anybody could ask tough questions from that chair . . .

Hema also appeared to be too fixed – there was just one way of doing things – the meeting was not going that well.

Soon the meeting progressed towards the grounds of productivity, efficiencies and yield – Ravi felt a little irritated, for there was a history behind the plant and the colony behind it – and this history was composed of blood and sweat, of sacrifices and great moments of togetherness, of accidents and of miracles . . . none of these appear on an Excel sheet or a SAP report.

Hema repeated the word *innovation* for the tenth time to get Ravi out of his own reveries . . . Ravi was not very fond of this word being used lightly and rather superficially thrown around.

His training as an engineer was invested into the notion of small improvements, of kaizen, and of looking at improving efficiency and yields diligently and with faith. There were times when the global vendor would be surprised and awed at what he and his team had accomplished; these were shared over a drink and never in a formal report to the CEO.

Ravi loved the prospect of getting his 'hands-on' technology – he loved pottering around at the Gemba – he disliked engineers and foremen who did not spend a lot of time at the plant. Greasy hands, sweaty shirts, and oily uniforms were a sign of really working with technology.

As the meeting drew towards closure, both Hema and Ravi were left with a sense of incomprehension and incompletion. Both were wondering whether the other person had understood him or her, the kind of impression they had made on each other and what kind of relationship are they going to have with this other person who was absolutely critical to their own success and future.

Part 2

Exploring Hema and Ravi through the EUM lens

The preceding scenario has been witnessed by us, quite often. It is not merely the modern multinationals but also the traditional Indian business houses that are feeling the need to integrate Ravi's ways (which have hitherto worked well) with Hema's approach, which seems more suitable to meet the demands of a fast-moving VUCA world. It is tempting to view the dynamics between Ravi and Hema as an inevitable conflict between tradition and modernity and/or as conflict between two "personality types". However, the issues involved may be a lot more complex.

Viewed through the EUM Lens, Ravi and Hema are not seen as two different "types" of people but as different configurations of the same basic elements. In that sense, both Hema and Ravi reside within each of us, and how they relate within ourselves has a profound impact on how we engage with them externally. This process becomes quite apparent when we look at the analysis of EUM data in the previous chapter.

It is easy to see that the self-concept of our respondents as reflected in the SC scores is very Ravi-like. If we relate them to the spiral given in Figure 3.1, we can see that there is a clear leaning towards the left side of the spiral (UBP, URB and UMI) as compared to the right side (USD and UPA) Thus, it would seem that, like Ravi, our respondents are likely to pay more attention to the relationship ambience and look at authority figures as "benevolent patriarchs" who need to "look after their people", "take interest in them" and "guide and direct them" in a "firm and fair" manner. They are likely to see themselves as pragmatic, down-to-earth and grounded in their context. Thus, they would be as flabbergasted as Ravi when they encounter someone like Hema who offers only a "perfunctory introduction about herself", does not "delve into his background", appears "more interested in numbers than people" and talks of "innovation" without having any idea of the "ground realities". To them Hema is likely to appear as callous, self-centered, overambitious and somewhat shallow.

Interestingly, this is precisely the picture, which our respondents draw of "other people" in their OP scores. In contrast to oneself, others are seen as leaning towards the right side of the spiral, for example, USD and UPA. As pointed out in the previous chapter, our respondents see other people as less concerned about "rules of the game" (URB), "humanistic values" (UMI), "lower in wisdom" (UDS) but more governed by "personal needs" (USD) and "ambition" (UPA)

We also find that in their own way, our respondents wish to become more Hema-like, as reflected in the desired shifts from SC to SI (increase in UPA and drop in UMI/URB). Simultaneously, there is no appreciable change in the USD scores. This suggests that our respondents want to embrace Hema's UPA but not her USD. While they may carry their disdain towards what they see as Hema's self-centricity, there is perhaps also a sneaking admiration for the freedom with which she seems to operate – a freedom that our respondents find difficult to give to themselves. They also seem to believe that at the heart of Hema's sense of freedom lies a disregard for humanistic values.

Thus, while they see themselves as shackled by humanistic values, they believe that the Hemas of this world have managed to get rid of them and perhaps are better off than themselves.

In order to explore this further, it would be helpful to understand the orientation of Indian managers towards three interrelated dimensions:

- Agency
- Structure
- Communion

Agency

The agentic orientation represents that part of ourselves that makes us feel like a "free bird" who can do as it wishes and who can go where its heart takes it. This is a part that wishes to gain mastery over our destiny, that propels us to discern and make choices and that makes us pursue our own needs, goals and desires. In the EUM framework, the agentic orientation is represented by USD and UPA. The systemic features that foster agency are Arena and Network.

Structure

The structural orientation represents that part of ourselves that seeks stability and security. This is a part of ourselves that propels us to give up some of our volition and freedom and to accept the dictates of the structure of which we are a part. It enables us to follow the rules and regulations laid down by the context and to adhere to the requisite systemic discipline. In the EUM framework this orientation is represented by UBP and URB. At the systemic level, this orientation is fostered by Clan and Clockwork.

Communion

The communion orientation is represented by that part of our selves that wishes to relate and that reminds us of our commonality and linkage to other people. It propels us to care about other people, empathize with them, relate to them meaningfully and contribute to their well-being. This connectedness may remain confined to people in one's immediate context or may extend to humanity at large.

In EUM framework, this orientation is represented by UBP and UMI. At the systemic level, the communion orientation is fostered by Universes of Clan and Ecological. When there is a preponderance of UBP, the communion orientation is directed towards one's own people, but when the leaning is towards UMI, the communion orientation is more generic and extended to outsiders as well.

Our data indicate that, like Ravi, Indian managers are high on structural orientation and moderate on agentic and communion orientation. Importantly, they believe that other people are relatively higher on agentic orientation but lower than them on structural and communion orientation. This is akin to Ravi's perception of Hema. They also seem to believe that their communion orientation is an obstacle in their wish to enhance their agentic orientation.

Consequently, rather than grace their relatively higher communion orientation and deploy it as a strength, they see it as a liability and wish to reduce it. The single largest drop from SC to SI in our sample is in UMI. Similarly, in EUM-O, *Ecological* drops appreciably from OC to OI. The operating principle seems to be that "since everyone else seems to be low on Communion orientation, so should I/We". Needless to say, this is a self-fulfilling prophecy whereby everyone rationalizes his or her own stance and behavior by projecting a low communion orientation onto others.

In this context, it is important to consider how the communion orientation is likely to manifest itself. Given the greater comfort of our respondents with UBP than UMI, the communion orientation is likely to have a greater UBP flavor (i.e., towards one's own people) rather than a UMI flavor (i.e., in terms of broader humanistic values) In this scenario, systemic responsibility is likely to be defined primarily in terms of one's immediate context, and therefore, the individual's relatedness with the immediate system of belonging will be very different from his or her relatedness with the larger system. The obvious implication of this is that the same action by the self will be seen as altruistic (I did it for the sake of my people) and as selfish in case of others (he or she is ONLY bothered about his or her own people).

In case of Hema and Ravi, what may seem like genuine care and concern for others to Ravi is likely to be seen as clannish and parochial by Hema. Thus, Ravi would see himself as someone who is trying to balance the needs of looking after people with task demands; to Hema, he will come through as a closed-minded person who is overprotective of his own people and turf with no concern for the larger picture.

This would push Ravi into believing that the only way out for him is to tone down his communion orientation, which is precisely what our respondents seem to be saying. Ironically, the attempt to enhance agentic orientation at the expense of communion orientation boomerangs on the individual, for it creates further isolation. Bereft of any emotional support and infrastructure, the person feels even more helpless and alone in dealing with the pushes and pulls of the situation.

The energy of the person gets focused on somehow coping with the multiple demands being made on him or her rather than acting from one's volition and conviction. Moreover, bereft of communion orientation, the individual loses an important source of legitimacy for exercising his or her agency. Many a Ravi are able to act with courage and conviction because they believe that they are acting on behalf of the system and not just for their personal gain. Once they let go of their communion orientation, ironically, they also say good-bye to their agency.

Even in the best of situations, while this stance does not impair the managerial effectiveness of the individual, it can become a serious impediment to actualization of their leadership potential. Exercising leadership entails deployment of either agentic orientation or communion orientation and preferably both. The present stance of the Indian manager does not help in standing up either for the Self or for the collective good. Often the individual becomes a medium through which things happen.

This accounts for the wide prevalence of the middle management syndrome (where the individual feels sandwiched between competing pressures from both ends) in Indian organizations at virtually all levels. We have often found very senior managers who are virtually at the top of the organizational hierarchy complain about "Management".

When we asked as to who exactly do they mean by "Management", we usually draw a blank or an evasive response. Our speculation is that the leadership function in Indian organizations is either attributed to one or two people at the top or assigned to an invisible entity called "Management". It rarely becomes a shared and lived experience.

Given the fast-moving and dynamic context in which they find themselves, a large part of the energy of our respondents gets expended in somehow coping with the multiple demands being placed on them rather than proactively shaping their context. It is therefore not surprising that, like Ravi, our respondents feel hugely "let down" by the "system". Their expectation is that the organization will create such conditions wherein they feel empowered, discover their agency and bring forth their creativity. However, in absence of these conditions they experience failed dependency and fall back on their own ingenuity in somehow coping with the situation by becoming *Jugaad* experts.

Jugaad experts

The term *Jugaad* has often been used in the context of Indianness. It is very difficult to find an English equivalent for *Jugaad* – it has shades of improvisation, expediency, patchwork, compromise, bending of rules, finding shortcuts and so on. Its essence is to somehow manage a tricky or seemingly impossible situation without upsetting the apple cart. In a scenario when things are breaking down, the individual makes a desperate attempt to prevent complete collapse and keep his or her head above water by deploying his or her ingenuity.

Indian managers are often required to deliver under difficult situations of resource constraints, poor infrastructure, unreasonable demands, crippling bureaucracy and the like. Simultaneously, their psychological orientation of low assertion, inability to stand up for their convictions, conflict avoidance and high structural orientation keeps pushing them into situations where they feel powerless to impact/influence the larger system and deal with the basic issues confronting them. Under the circumstances the best that they can do is to somehow cope with the situation by deploying their ingenuity through Jugaad.

While Jugaad helps them to take care of the "urgent", it is often at the cost of "important". The obvious implication of this is that while symptoms are taken care of, the basic issues remain unaddressed. Thus, the individual never feels on top of the situation.

Once some of us had been invited by an organization to address what they considered as lack of collaboration in the senior management team. As we discussed their context, we learned that the organization had recently received substantial financial investment from an external source. In order to attract this funding, the growth projections had been exaggerated very substantially. Naturally, the new investor was now demanding that these promises be delivered. Consequently, each member of the top management team was under tremendous pressure to deliver on these highly unreasonable targets. Each of them was doing his or her bit of Jugaad with no concern about what it may do to the others. While the HR head could see the symptom of "inadequate collaboration", he was not willing to acknowledge the more basic issues, let alone address them. Clearly, he was also doing his bit of Jugaad by organizing a few team-building workshops that could, at least temporarily, take the focus away from this internal chaos and create some sense of well-being, no matter how fragile it may be. In our experience, a large number of such interventions are of Jugaad variety, which rather than addressing the issues merely pushes them under the carpet.

In many ways, Jugaad represents both the "best" and the "worst" side of Indian managers. On one hand, it shows their ingenuity, resilience and flexibility, and on the other hand, it shows their propensity to compromise, their unwillingness to confront and their readiness to sacrifice the "important" for the sake of the "urgent". One cannot help wondering, "What if the strengths of ingenuity, resilience, adaptability and the like were deployed in service of their conviction rather than in merely coping with their situation?"

For this to happen, a healthy integration between Ravi and Hema is absolutely critical. Our experience suggests that whenever the two are in sync with each other, understand each other and see the other as a resource, they produce magical results. On the other hand, when they get caught in an adversarial relationship, what ensues is tremendous waste and dysfunctional conflicts. Often, this uneasy relationship is not just between two people but also within the individual him- or herself.

Till Ravi is able to acknowledge and grace the Hema within himself, the external Hema will only appear as pushy, aggressive, selfish, overambitious and noncaring. Similarly, for Hema to see Ravi in his own right, she will need to ask what she has done with Ravi within herself. In absence of this she will only see Ravi as an old-school, closed-minded, clannish fossil who has outlived his utility. For either of them to be able to do this, they will need to engage with the more basic question about what they have done with their civilizational codings. This is so because the unease between Ravi and Hema is borne out of the uneasy relationship between the civilizational codings of the Indian psyche and the imperatives of the corporate world.

In the last chapter, we look at what a meaningful co-holding of the two is likely to entail. However, in order to that, we first need to delve deeper into the civilizational codings of the Indian manager and how they manifest in the corporate world.

Note

1 Many in India do not get admission into an engineering college and then opt for a diploma course that is considered a much inferior certification.

Chapter 6

Civilizational codings
of Indian managers

Introducing the notion of the
civilizational identity

As mentioned in the Introduction of this book, civilizations differ
from each other with respect to not just their customs and practices
but also in terms of their beliefs and assumptions about human
existence. Simultaneously, there is much in common between them
because they have to deal with the same human imperatives. The
differences lie in each civilization's unique way of engaging with
these imperatives.

Thus, the uniqueness of a civilization cannot be understood in
terms of absolutes of mutually exclusive categories. Instead, it has to
be seen as a relative emphasis or tilt in dealing with dualities that may
have a contrary pull. One civilization may place greater emphasis
on "contentment" whereas another may be more driven by "ambition". Similarly, some civilizations may be more individual-centric
whereas some others may be more community-centric. While talking of civilizational identity, it is important to remember that the
idea is not to stereotype but only to acknowledge the nuances that
stem from civilizational uniqueness. This is even more important in
the Indian context because of its huge diversity and major discontinuities in its geopolitical history.

The Indian context

There are some obvious difficulties with the concept of civilizational identity in the Indian context. To begin with, there is a huge
diversity of religion, language, caste, class, customs etc. Hence the
common threads, if any, are not immediately visible and extremely

difficult to validate empirically. There are strong stereotypes associated with different regions (e.g., Punjabis are supposed to be
aggressive and zestful, Bengalis are supposed to be sensitive and
artistic, South Indians are supposed to be more devout and so on).
Similar stereotypes exist across different religions and class/caste
categories. It has sometimes been argued that India is nothing more
than a geopolitical entity – a convenient coalition of diverse groups,
which came together postindependence. In such a scenario does the
notion of a civilizational identity have any relevance?

Linked to the preceding point is the issue of significant discontinuities in Indian history, for example, Colonial rule. All civilizations
go through both continuities and discontinuities. When the movement is characterized by continuities, the essential character of the
civilization is easily identified with and almost taken for granted
by its citizens. However, the story is quite different when it comes
to discontinuities. Each discontinuity leaves its mark on the collective psyche, making it extremely difficult to distinguish between its
"essential characteristic" and a "coping mechanism".

Thus, a question about the real character of the civilization
becomes akin to asking as to what is the real character of a river –
at the point of origin, when it passes through lush green planes,
when it encounters hilly terrains or when it merges with the ocean?
It is tempting to look at only the "here and now" and the present
context, but this could be misleading particularly if one only looks
at the manifest and not at what lies beneath the tip of the iceberg. In
other words, the behavioral patterns and traits being displayed may
be essentially "contextual" and/or ways of dealing with the present
situation. They may not be of much help (and may even mislead)
in our attempt to understand the intrinsic nature of Indian Identity.

Another significant difficulty arises from the fact that the
"secondary socialization" (education, work systems, etc.) of many
Indians is in frames that may broadly be called "Western". The
influence of these frames in our education systems and design of
workspaces is quite strong. This is particularly true of most people
in our sample who come from an urban, educated upper-/middle-
class, English-speaking backgrounds. Their contact with Indian
heritage rarely goes beyond following a few rituals, celebrating
some festivals (often without knowing their origin and significance) and an ambivalent relationship with the so-called Indian
values (e.g., respect for age/tradition, selflessness, contentment,
non-violence, motherhood, chastity, spiritual endeavor, etc.).

Often, they not merely experience a huge gap between these values and their actual experience of Indian reality; they may also see these values as deterrents to their aspirations for progress and advancement. Not surprisingly expressions like "Indian Womanhood" invite more derision than reverence from many of them. Furthermore, their personal connection is generally restricted to "their own kind" and, hence, excludes the vast majority of other Indians with whom their link is essentially "transactional" in nature and remains devoid of any emotive/personal dimension. While this restricted contact is true of most social groups, it is perhaps more pronounced in India because of tighter segregation across class and caste. Thus, one can question whether these people really represent the quintessential Indian character.

In view of the various factors listed, our approach has been to go beyond the manifest behavior and personality traits and focus on the underlying beliefs and values about human existence and relationships. Our hypothesis is that beneath the diversity of class, caste, education, social status, religion and language and so on, there is an invisible thread of what may broadly be called the "Indian way". A telling example of this commonality is the tremendous hold that the "caste system" has in the Indian society. Interestingly, one can find it prevalent even amongst people whose religion specifically prohibits it (e.g., Islam, Christianity, Sikhism, etc.).

The advancement in education levels has not made any significant impact on it. One only has to see the "matrimonial column" of any Indian newspaper (including English newspapers, which are presumably read by the more educated and modernized Indians) across the country to experience the all-pervasive hold that the caste system has on the Indian psyche. Our hypothesis is that this "hold of the caste system" has much less to do with either religion or superstition but should be understood in the context of the "hold of the belonging system" as well as preoccupations with hierarchy and purity/pollution in the Indian identity. In India, for most people, irrespective of their caste, class, religion and so on, their "belonging system" is a significant anchor of their identity. Beyond the immediate family, this "belonging system" is represented by what is commonly referred to as *Jati*

In this sense, the notion of jati is not confined to any specific religious group or economic class. For most people adherence to the rules, norms and boundaries of their Jati or *Biradari* (community of belonging) is a strong imperative. Thus, the individual, irrespective of his or her religion, educational background, economic status and the like, experiences a strong compulsion to stay within the boundaries laid down by his or her Jati or Biradari, which provides the necessary impetus to its grip over the individual.

Keeping all these factors in mind, what we offer in the following is our understanding of the underlying beliefs and orientations of the Indian civilizational identity. These are speculative in nature and not empirically verified/verifiable. They are partly based on our own experience and partly on the insights gained from several scholars, particularly Shri Ashis Nandy, Dr. Pulin K. Garg, Shri Dharampal and Dr. Sudhir Kakkar.

In many places, we have not specifically referred to these scholars, though the ideas have been inspired by them. Since these are our interpretations of their ideas, they may not reflect their intent. Consequently, references have been provided only when we are specifically quoting them. At a more general level we can only express our indebtedness to them for their inspiration.

In our understanding, some of the main features of the Indian identity are as follows.

I. "I" OR "ME"

George Herbert Mead made an important distinction between I and Me.[1] He postulated that every human being is both an individualistic and innovative being (I) and a social and relational being (Me). These two interdependent aspects are part of every human being and create an inevitable dualistic polarity particularly between the need for autonomy and the need for belonging. In the EUM framework, this duality is represented by the two sides of the spiral. The right side (USD and UPA) represents the I orientation, whereas the left side (UBP, URB and UMI) represents the ME orientation.

As can be seen from the analysis of the EUM data, the Indian identity leans more towards the Me (belonging) rather than I (autonomy)

Thus, in the Indian identity, system of belonging has a very special place. The question, "Who am I?" is invariably translated into "Where do I come from", that is, which family, which caste, which community, which village, which province, which educational institution and so on, and "What are my current affiliations", that is, where do I work, which clubs/social institutions that I belong to, what are my religious affiliations and so on.

In other words, an individual is primarily defined by his or her affiliations. Other considerations like capabilities, preferences, needs/desires, goals/aspirations, beliefs and values are of relatively less importance. This primacy of the belonging system gives a special force to the imperatives of the belonging system. The dos and don'ts of the belonging system are experienced as strong "musts" by the individual, and he or she finds it difficult to break free from them. Earlier, we suggested that the primacy of belonging system has much to do with the strong hold of the caste system in the Indian society. Additionally, there are many other consequences. Some of these include the following:

a   Given the primacy of the belonging system, it becomes extremely important for the individual to know his or her "exact place" in the system – what is expected of him or her, and what can he or she expect from others. What are the boundaries that must be adhered to, and what is the leeway that he or she has? It is therefore not surprising that URB ranks at the very top in the SC of our respondents. Consequently, role ambiguity creates discomfort and fluid structures become a source of anxiety for the individual. When put in such situations, the individual tends to fall back on "groups of familiarities" (based on common background of region, religion, caste/class, etc.) in order to experience a sense of safety and security. This process comes quite naturally to us, given our comfort with UBP. Hence, strong affiliative groups based on village, caste, community and the like are a fairly common feature of most Indian organizations. Even in modern-day multinationals, which are primarily based on matrix structures and network cultures, it is not uncommon to find a parallel informal structure that is primarily of a clan culture. Thus, what on paper seems like a Network organization is often a collation of clans that have found some ways to coexist peacefully.

b   The notion of personal responsibility in the Indian psyche is primarily defined in relation to the immediate system of belonging (family, clan, work groups, etc.) and role imperatives. The communion orientation in the Indian psyche has a much stronger UBP flavor (concern for one's own people) rather than a UMI flavor (concern for humanistic values). Thus, while the individual has a strong commitment to his or her own people, the larger system generally remains a depersonalized and diffused entity. The operative belief is that so long as one has done one's bit, one need not worry about the larger system and that it will somehow take care of itself. Thus, it is not uncommon to find that we Indians are generally immune to any guilt feelings when it comes to our membership of the larger system. Preoccupation with purity of one's personal space (e.g., home) and polluting public spaces (e.g., streets) with impunity is a fairly common phenomenon. In work systems, this manifests through a strong commitment to one's own work group/section/department and relative indifference to the larger context. Similarly, violation of systemic discipline and use of systemic privileges for the benefit of oneself and one's immediate context are generally regarded as the done thing. In fact, a person who does not use his or her personal position for the benefit of his or her family and clan is more likely to be despised as self-centered rather than being revered as a fair person. This indifference towards the larger system also contributes to insensitivity to social inequities and injustices.

Overall, the primacy of the belonging system creates a situation wherein the individual is likely to surrender completely to the imperatives of the immediate context and disregard the responsibility towards the larger system. In either case, any meaningful negotiation with the system becomes extremely difficult. While the immediate context remains the primary source of belonging and protection, it is also seen as restrictive and suffocating. On the other hand, the larger system is seen as hostile and unjust but simultaneously as a "free-for-all" space where one can not only pursue opportunities but also discharge pent-up rage. Thus, it is not uncommon to find some of the most privileged Indians carrying grouse and bitterness about being discriminated against and not receiving their due.

Simply put, the Indian psyche is highly prone towards oscillating between being a "puppet" in the immediate context and a "loose cannon" in the larger context. This is particularly important in the context of the fact that most modern-day organizations are built on the principle of "responsible agency and pursuit of self-interest", which does not come very easily to us.

c   The Me orientation and the emphasis on the sanctity of roles and boundaries create a strong link between personal honor and role appropriateness. Any deviation from role appropriateness (even if it be in thought/feeling and not translated into action) becomes a trigger for shame and loss of personal honor. Since it is virtually impossible for any individual to have only role appropriate feelings, the triggers for shame are ever present in the Indian scenario.

In psychoanalytical terms, shame is associated with the pre-Oedipal stage and linked to "fear of abandonment". It is significant to note that in most parts of traditional Indian society, the most prevalent way of dealing with deviant behavior was through "*Hukka Paani Band*", that is, exclusion from the circle of social intercourse. In subtler ways, the same principle is deployed in the modern-day urban society and even the corporate world, where exclusion from the informal groups becomes a powerful message of peer disapproval.

In such a scenario, the individual remains hugely dependent on the approval of people in the immediate group for his or her self-worth. The individual's ability to affirm him- or herself remains low, and there is a constant need to seek affirmation/ reassurance from outside, particularly from people who are higher in status. This is often accompanied by a hypersensitivity to "public slight", "loss of face" and defensiveness against real or imagined criticism/disapproval. On the other hand, sometimes this preoccupation is engaged with complete denial and a defiant stance of "I don't care". In either case, acting from conviction becomes difficult. One either complies with "expectations of other" or out of a defiant disregard but rarely from a perspective that is based on one's own reflection and deliberation.

d Perhaps in most rural agrarian societies, there is a huge overlap between the primary system (family and other systems of belonging) and the secondary system (workplace and other systems of performance/instrumentality). In the Indian context, it may be even more pronounced because of the caste system in which the social identity of the person is coterminous with work/professional identity. It therefore becomes difficult for most Indians to look at the workplace as a depersonalized entity, which is only governed by instrumental considerations of merit, performance, contribution and so on. The affiliative considerations have an equally strong pull.

In many organizations one often comes across the expression "We are just like a family here". The implicit message of this statement is "All is well if there is emotional bonding between people". Thus, considerable emphasis is placed on establishing "personal rapport" in all task relationships. When a significant senior person leaves an organization, often several people close to him or her follow suit. In such a context, constructs like teamwork, superior–subordinate relationship and performance management, among others, carry a unique emotive flavor that mostly remains below the surface. What is visible at the surface level is only the tip of the iceberg, and ignoring what lies beneath can have disastrous consequences and leave one with a sense of incomprehension. For example, while issues are deliberated through logic and exchange of ideas, it is the underlying dynamics of relationships that determine the course of this surface-level rationality. It is therefore not surprising that most of our respondents see themselves as more "rational" than others; presumably the underlying "irrationality" of others is seen more easily than one's own.

e Another consequence of the ME orientation is that the individual derives his or her sense of security from the network of relationships rather than from competence and contribution. This is not to suggest that Indians do not invest in their competence but only that no matter how competent the person is, the network of his or her relationships remains the primary anchor of security. In fact, in the course of our engagements with several organizations, we often come across highly competent people who start feeling very destabilized if there is any disturbance in their relationship with significant others. A direct consequence of this is that rewards are seen as acts of bestowal rather than as something that the individual has earned. Similarly, it becomes very difficult to distinguish differentiation from discrimination.

f The greater leaning towards the relational orientation also means that informal norms and social processes, such as inclusion/exclusion or approval/disapproval, have a stronger impact on individual behavior than do formal rules and regulations.

In the traditional Indian social design, the balance of power among individual, society and state was heavily tilted in favor of the society. The individual's freedom was limited, and so was the intervention from the state. By and large, communities were self-governing, and the task of regulating individual behavior was performed by each community on the basis of its established principles, practices and norms. It is therefore not surprising that, by and large, Indians have a higher "social sense" than "civic sense". What other people will think/feel about them and the social consequences of their actions become more important than "rule of law".

In sharp contrast to this, the modern-day societies are built on the primacy of "individual liberty". The basic belief is that so long as the individual does not infringe on the freedom of others, he or she should have complete freedom to choose and act according to his or her own preferences, beliefs and values. In this scenario, the society becomes redundant, and the role of the state gets confined to ensuring adherence to "rule of law".

The tension between "rule of law" and "social dynamics" can be witnessed in several areas of modern-day life. At the macro-social level, it gets manifested in areas such as inter-caste relations, gender relations, religious/traditional practices and so on. Even the corporate life is not free of this tension. Conducting a disciplinary action proceeding is not merely an exercise of determining adherence/violation of rules but also an engagement with the ramifications on social dynamics.

What this also means is that notions such as "autocratic" and "democratic" have a very different flavor in the Indian context. Exercising unilateral power/authority is rarely seen as auto-cratic, provided it is done with sensitivity to the social dynam-ics. On the other hand, even legitimate exercising of power and authority will be experienced as oppressive/tyrannical if it dis-turbs the existing social equilibrium. Thus, someone like Ravi may not be seen as autocratic because even when acting in a unilateral manner, he would keep the social dynamics in mind. On the other hand, Hema is more likely to be seen as autocratic and bossy, because of her scant regard for the social reality.

The following observation made by Pulin Garg captures the difficulty in working with concepts of authoritarian/democratic leadership in India:

> It is often found that authoritarian behavior reflects demo-cratic processes and democratic behavior imposes authoritar-ian processes. Even F- scale values of the individual do not find support from the clinical data of the same individual.[2]

2. Context sensitivity

In a brilliant essay titled "Is There an Indian Way of Thinking",[3] the well-known poet and scholar, A. R. Ramanujan, has suggested that context sensitivity is the preferred mode in Indian culture.

Ramanujan begins by drawing our attention to a commonly held belief about Indian character, namely, inconsistency. Inconsistency is a trait often associated with Indians. A reputed magazine had once invited several intellectuals to talk about Indian character. Not surprisingly, hypocrisy appeared on almost everyone's list. Ramanujan talks of his own difficulty in understanding how his father could hold both astronomy and astrology in the same brain. As he says, "I looked for consistency in him, a consistency he didn't seem to care about".

Another feature towards which he draws our attention is the absence of Universality. In Indian ethics, there are no absolutes like "Thou shall not kill" or presumption of universal applicability of a principle. He provides the following quote from Hegel to illustrate this: "While we may say 'Bravery is a virtue', the Hindoos say 'Bravery is a virtue of the Cshatriyas' ".[4]

Ramanujan argues that these features are not a result of a deficiency in logical thinking, an underdeveloped ego strength or a deficient morality but because of a fundamentally different approach to contextuality. He states,

I think cultures (may be said to) have overall tendencies (for whatever complex reasons)- the tendencies to idealise, and think in terms of, either the Context-free or the Context-sensitive kind of rules. Actual behavior may be more complex, though the rules they think with are a crucial factor in guiding the behavior. In cultures like India's, the context sensitive kind of rule is preferred formulation.

(Ramanujam 1989)

This context sensitivity can be experienced in virtually all spheres of Indian life – codes of ethics, literature, art forms and even daily interactions. If a survey were to be undertaken, it is highly likely that Indians would emerge as the highest users of the expression "it depends". Even the notion of Dharma (righteous conduct) for an Indian is contextual. It is determined by one's stage in life (*Asramdharma*),[5] one's innate nature and belonging (*Swadharma*)[6] and the specific demands of the situation (*Apaddharma*).[7]

In most Indian literary and art forms, considerable emphasis is given to context setting. Even time and space are not treated as neutral entities but are associated with specific contextual properties. Thus, each Raga[8] in Indian classical music is associated with specific time and season. Spaces are supposed to have their own auras, and times are auspicious or inauspicious depending on the event/activity involved. This context sensitivity can also be seen in everyday transactions. Cognitive anthropologist Richard Shweder[9] found significant differences in the way an Indian describes a person as compared to an American. The American is likely to describe the person in generic terms such as good, helpful, selfish and so on. In contrast, the Indian's description is likely to be more context-specific and behavioral; that is, this is what he or she did to so-and-so in such a situation. Thus, when you ask a person about anyone or anything, the response is likely to be in the form of an anecdote or a story.

Since for most Indians, the most important element of the context is their family, it is not surprising that Alan Roland[10] found that "Indians carry their family wherever they go". The truth of Roland's statement will easily resonate with anyone who has taken a train journey in India. In all likelihood, by the end of the journey the individual will be familiar with the complete family history of his or her co-passengers.

This context sensitivity is closely linked to what Ashis Nandy has called a "controlled schism between Existential consciousness (Atman) and attribute consciousness (Ego)".[11] In his book *The Intimate Enemy*, Nandy has narrated an episode about a group of 15th-century Aztec priests who were herded together as sorcerers by their Spanish conquerors. In response to a Christian sermon, the Aztec priests responded that "if as alleged, the Aztec gods were dead, they too would rather die". After this last act of defiance, the priests were dutifully thrown to the war dogs but simultaneously praised and respected for their courageous heroism by their conquerors.

Nandy goes on to speculate as to how a group of Brahmin priests would have acted under the same circumstances. His speculation (and we tend to agree with him) is that all of them would have embraced Christianity, but their faith in Hinduism would have remained unshaken, and in due course, their Christianity would have looked like a variation of Hinduism. They would have also perfectly justified and seen their action as *"Apad-dharma"* (righteous conduct under perilous conditions)

Viewed through the narrow lens of masculine values, the act of Aztec priests seems heroic and courageous whereas that of the hypothetical Brahmins as cowardly and hypocritical. However, Nandy invites us to consider how this peculiar mix of "overt compliance" and "inner resilience" enabled our civilization to survive over centuries and how it is a product of a deep-seated faith that no matter what happens to the physical, emotional and mental self, the "essential constituents" of the self can remain unaffected and untouched. This controlled schism between existential consciousness (Atman) and attribute consciousness (Ego), instead of threatening mental health, contributes to a peculiar robust realism.

Our hypothesis is that this controlled schism between existential and attribute consciousness is a significant source of the flexibility in the Indian identity that enables it to adapt to a context without losing its essential character. Hence, the individual can remain anchored in him- or herself and yet be able to adjust and adapt to the situational requirements.

Simultaneously, this schism can also become problematic if the schism between "inner resilience" and "overt compliance" becomes a "way of life" rather than just a response to a perilous situation. We suspect that this may well have happened in case of the Indian identity, particularly in view of the historical traumas that the Indian civilization has been through. It is now not just *Apad-dharma* but almost a "way of life" as well. Thus, what a person "says" may be very different from what he or she may actually "think or feel".

Withholding of disagreement (particularly with a person who is higher in status) is a fairly common feature in Indian organizations, families and even social settings. Similarly, often service providers would make commitments that they know are impossible to keep. Paying lip service to ideas such as gender diversity and keeping one's reservations to oneself are common features. Consequently, there is an ambiguity about the intent of the "other" as well as uncertainty about what one can realistically expect from the other. Not surprisingly, most of our respondents find their organizations as "overly diplomatic" and other people as more tactful than themselves.

A significant implication of this simultaneity of inner resilience with overt compliance is that while the Indian psyche is extremely open and flexible at the surface level, it is also deeply anchored in its own beliefs and convictions. However, this deep anchorage often manifests as an unstated rigidity that resists any real impact or influence. It is likely that this is a defensive strategy used by the Indian psyche to preserve its own integrity in the face of external attacks and invasions. Thus, it easily includes many things without actually assimilating them. The Indian civilization has often been compared to a flowing river that takes in whatever comes its way and/or is thrown into it. People with diverse backgrounds have come into this land and made it into their home. Similarly, ideas, practices, religious beliefs, art forms and living habits that may have originated elsewhere find a reasonably comfortable place in India. However, this inclusivity does not necessarily mean assimilation or integration. Quite often, these indiscriminately swallowed elements remain as fragments without becoming an integrated part of the whole. As in the example of the hypothetical Brahmins stated earlier, Christianity may be embraced at the surface level, but its true spirit may not be assimilated.

The Indian social and professional life is full of such surface-level inclusion. The way an urban middle-/upper-class Indian dresses, talks and lives is almost indistinguishable from his or her Western counterparts. This modernity/Westernization is often a surface-level phenomenon. Scratch the surface and you are like to discover a mind-set that is deeply entrenched in tradition. Similarly, in the professional sphere concepts and techniques are readily included from the outside but rarely implemented in their true spirit. Sophisticated systems of performance management are incorporated but actual people related decisions are based on affiliative considerations.

In this sense, we seem to have reversed what Macaulay[12] wished us to become. His attempt was to create a set of people who are "outwardly Indian" but think like a "Westerner". Instead, we seem to have become a set of people who are outwardly Westernized but think like Indians.

This is not to suggest that the experience of colonization has not affected our psyche. It most certainly has, but the impact has been more in the nature of fragmenting the psyche rather than transforming it. The fragmentation happens because often the Western frames are indiscriminately swallowed without paying any attention to their underlying assumptions, beliefs and values. Sadly, in this process we become alienated from our own ways without deriving the benefit of that which we have taken in.

Thus, while we have been able to incorporate the form of democracy, the assimilation of democratic values remains a distant dream. The issue of secularism is even more complex. While we have swallowed the idea of separating religion from politics and governance, the mutual respect and sensitivity to different religions have diminished rather than enhanced. It is rarely recognized that the idea of secularism that we have swallowed arose primarily in the context of conflict between temporal/state authority and religious/spiritual authority and not for enhancing mutual respect among different faiths. Thus, it is possible that in the process of this indiscriminate swallowing, some of our traditional ways of "coexistence" have also been jettisoned, and all that we are left with is a reactive backlash.

A significant implication of this process of "inclusion without assimilation" is that systems rarely become "coherent wholes". Mostly, they remain a collation of fragmented subsystems, which have learned to coexist and transact with each other in a reasonably functional way. In a way, this was the basic model on which the traditional rural society was organized – a collation of subcommunities with clearly laid out rules and boundaries of transaction across them. Thus, Hindus and Moslems could peacefully coexist in the same village so long as they observed the requisite prohibitions particularly in the sphere of inter-dining and intermarriage.

This phenomenon was beautifully captured by Mani Ratnam in his film *Bombay*.[13] The film opens with depicting the life in a village where the Hindu and Moslem communities coexist in a harmonious and amiable manner. However, all hell breaks loose when a Hindu boy falls in love with a Moslem girl.

Thus, in the Indian context, "salad bowl" as a metaphor of integration has much greater applicability than "melting pot". Unlike in a melting pot, in the salad bowl, each constituent retains its own identity and yet becomes a meaningful part of a coherent whole. Thus, integration at the cost of the autonomy and integrity of any subsystem often becomes a point of contention. At the macrosociopolitical level, it is manifested through resistance to ideas like "uniform civil code". At the micro level of organizational functioning, it manifests through the need to address the salient features of each subsystem in any organization-wide intervention.

As stated earlier, civilizational quintessence is a matter of emphasis and not a water-tight categorization. Thus, context sensitivity is only a cultural preference – it is not that Indians don't or can't think in a context-free manner or that people from other civilizations don't think in context-sensitive ways; it is merely a matter of relative emphasis. Also, there is nothing inherently superior or inferior about either of the two modalities – they are just two different ways of thinking. However, they have their unique prerequisites and implications.

Context-free rules are much more definitive as compared to context-sensitive rules that necessarily have to take many nuances into account. Consequently, context sensitivity requires higher tolerance for ambiguity. Also, it entails much greater reliance on subjective wisdom whereas context-free thinking relies more on objective facts and universal principles. In case of context-free frames, it is relatively simpler to lay down rules that can be followed uniformly. Context sensitivity entails juggling with multiple factors and variables that are not always very easy to codify. It is thus not surprising that Indians tend to rely much more on wisdom and experience rather than knowledge and rule books.

Reverence for "holy men" in India does not flow only from spiritual leanings but also from greater association of wisdom and consequent guru-dom with them. Consultation with family gurus for all kinds of matters (including financial, marital, family disputes, etc.) is a fairly common practice. Even in modern-day organizations, our experience suggests that coaches are often treated as gurus rather than as professional experts. Thus, coaching, in the Indian context, is generally a more "free-flowing" dialog than a structured transaction.

Similarly, there is much greater reliance on the subjective wisdom of authority figures both in personal and professional spaces. This can be viewed as immature dependency, but when seen from the perspective of the concerned individual, it is essentially a willingness to go by the "subjective wisdom" of someone who is presumed to have greater experience in juggling with multiple variables that are inherent in context sensitivity. The difficulty arises when this "willing acceptance" is replaced by the complete abdication of responsibility to think for oneself.

Whether we look at it as "willing acceptance" or "complete abdication", it can only operate on a foundation of solid trust and faith, particularly in authority relationships. Thus, loyalty of the subordinate and good will of the superior are of utmost importance in authority relationships in the Indian situation. So long as the subordinate believes that the superior will act in the best interest of the subordinate, he or she will easily accept the inconsistencies of the boss and attribute his or her boss with greater experience/wisdom – "the boss knows better" or "must be having very good reasons for this inconsistency" kind of syndrome.

If we revisit the case of Ravi and Hema, we can see that Ravi, who operates with a context-sensitive frame, would be surprised by Hema's indifference to the context and jumping into numbers and targets as though they exist in a vacuum. Similarly, Hema, who operates with a context-free frame, would get irritated by Ravi's insistence on delving into the context while she would much rather have him engaged on the matter at hand of targets and expectations. Also, Ravi's notions of authority as a benevolent and wise figure would clash with her notions, which are more likely to be configured on an adult-to-adult relationship.

The natural Indian propensity towards context sensitivity requires faith in subjective wisdom both of self and others. However, when the individual finds him- or herself surrounded by people whom he or she is not sure of, it becomes extremely difficult to operate with any sense of conviction.

Add to this the fact that the education of most Indians has been in context-free frames and the large/complex systems that they belong to are based on context-free principles. These systems place greater emphasis on objective analysis and uniform/consistent application of universal principles rather than subjective wisdom. Thus, whenever subjective wisdom is exercised by oneself it is seen as a necessary coping mechanism, but when it is exercised by others it is seen as ad hoc–ism, hypocrisy and expediency. The end result is that that the person perpetually finds him- or herself in a perilous situation in which he or she has to find ingenious ways to keep his or her head above water. Thus, as suggested earlier, Apaddharma seems to have become a way of life wherein one finds oneself caught in a never-ending chain of stressful and threatening situations. No wonder, the Indian managers are often regarded as Jugaad experts.

3. Preoccupation with hierarchy

As mentioned earlier if there is one feature which cuts across all differences of region, religion and language, in India, it is the caste system. Everyone condemns it but most people surrender to its dictates nevertheless. It has smuggled its way even in religions like Islam, Sikhism, Christianity and so on that specifically prohibit it. Under the circumstances, it seems reasonable to assume that the caste system has an intimate link with the Indian psyche. Our hypothesis is that the two main elements of this link are the following:

- Primacy of belonging system
- Preoccupation with hierarchy and its association with purity–pollution

While exploring the duality of I and Me, we examined the implications of the primacy of belonging system. We will now look at the second feature viz. preoccupation with hierarchy and associated dynamics of purity and pollution.

Few people will disagree with the proposition that Indians are highly status conscious people. Almost all cross-cultural studies (Hofstede, GLOBE research project) [14]have put India as a high-power distance culture, that is, having a large gap between power, authority and prestige among people.

Perhaps there are more very important persons (VIPs) in India than the rest of the world put together. "*Jante nahi mein kaun hoon?*" (Don't you know who I am?) is one of the most frequently used dialogs in Indian cinema. Postmatch ceremonies in India always have a large contingent on the dais, and the roles assigned to each person are governed by a clear pecking order. Any person even of modest social status expects to be treated like a VIP when interacting with people who he/she regards as lower in status than him- or herself. The wife of the CEO is the obvious choice for being the president of the wives' club. In any formal or informal group setting, the body language is so clear and obvious that the pecking order of people concerned stands out a mile. All in all, where one stands in relation to the other person with respect to status is of profound importance to most Indians. Furthermore, the relationship is generally defined in terms of higher or lower and very rarely as equal.

The association of hierarchy with purity–pollution assigns a certain sacredness to it whereby the person who is higher in the pecking order is also regarded as a superior human being – wiser, more evolved, more respectable and, hence, less governed by baser human instincts. On the other hand, people who are lower in the pecking order also become lesser human beings (*chhote log*) and, hence, of dubious character.

Often, the kind of family the individual comes from becomes a significant determinant of his or her culpability in any wrongful act – belonging to a respectable (i.e., higher in the pecking order) family is regarded as a certificate of good character and conduct. He or she comes from a good and respectable family is often used as a defense not just in social discourse but even in formal settings. Similarly, a wrongful act on part of a person belonging to the higher echelons is regarded as more despicable and a disgrace for the entire family/belonging system, whereas a similar act from a lower-ranked person would be regarded as "par for the course".

The preoccupation with hierarchy and its associated sacredness has significant implications for exercising power and authority. To a large extent these processes are not unique to India but are fairly universal. The only difference is that they are more pronounced in the Indian context.

In our experience with organizations (particularly in India) we have found that often hierarchy and authority become indistinguishable from each other. Authority is a structural construct whereby certain power is delegated to a role holder for effective task performance. For example, a police person is delegated the authority to regulate and control traffic movement. The status hierarchy of the role holder is of no consequence to his or her exercising this authority. Hierarchy, on the other hand, is based on the assumption of an unquestionable and absolute source of authority (say, a sacred text or a monarch), and the relative power is determined by the proximity to this source of absolute authority. In a hierarchy, it is assumed that the authority of any role holder can be usurped by someone who is higher in status. This is clearly absurd when applied to a task-based structure. For example, one cannot argue that the principal of a school should have the authority to overrule the decision of his or her teacher just because the principal happens to have a higher position in the status hierarchy. However, this simple principle that a role holder derives his or her authority from the structure and not from his or her boss is often not easily grasped by many people, and there is a widespread misconception that the authority of a role holder also rests with his or her boss and can be undermined by the boss at his or her sweet will.

A significant implication of associating authority with hierarchy and dynamics of purity and pollution is that hierarchy carries with it not just a set of privileges but also a set of prohibitions. It is therefore expected that people who are higher in the status hierarchy are also more restrained and circumspect in the way they conduct themselves. Liberties (in the sense of licentiousness), which may be permissible at lower levels, are denied to them (e.g., it is OK for a lower-caste person to behave in an unruly fashion but not for a higher-caste person). Failure to do so can lead to loss of respect and, hence, dilution of one's authority. In the Indian context, respect gets intricately linked with and often becomes the primary source of legitimacy for exercising authority.

If a person is respected, then it is assumed that he or she has legitimate right to exercise authority. Similarly, a loss of respect is tantamount to loss of authority. Not surprisingly, most Indian managers are hypersensitive about the respect that they believe is due to them from their subordinates. Admission of vulnerability or limitations in presence of people who are seen as "lower" is unthinkable for most Indians, and thus, "how could you say/do this to me in front of so and so?" becomes a major point of contention.

The other side of this preoccupation is that most people are forced to hide their normal human angularities/frailties in presence of people who they regard as lower than themselves. This process can be easily witnessed in both parent–child relationships and boss–subordinate relationships. In both cases, the essential fear is that any sign of human frailty will compromise the authority of the parent/boss. Coupled with the valuing of age and experience arising out of context sensitivity, discussed earlier, a high degree of reverence towards authority figures is inevitable. Simultaneously, when the authority figure fails to live up to this "larger-than-life" picture, there is a huge sense of "letdown" and cynicism.

Confusion between hierarchy and authority also creates huge difficulties in exercising upward or lateral authority. In view of the strong classification of role relationships and their linkage with seniority, peerage is not an easy proposition in the Indian context. Everyone is either higher or lower in role hierarchy. Since it is also assumed that authority can only be exercised with people who are inferior to oneself in the hierarchy, it becomes difficult for Indian managers to empower themselves in relation to their peers and superiors. Perhaps, this process has some bearing on the feeling of our respondents that their organizations are overly hierarchical and not as empowering as they should be.

What this also means is that one's status is determined by the accident of birth order rather than by one's own competence and achievement. Even when the individual is clearly more competent, his or her higher status is attributed to the birth order. In case of a family-owned business that we know of, the eldest brother is head and shoulders above his siblings in terms of his competence. However, the feeling amongst the younger siblings is that his higher position has been bestowed on him because of the chance occurrence of his being the eldest rather than being earned by him. Even in professionally managed organizations, competitiveness turns into sibling rivalry with great emphasis on relative proximity to the authority figure, who, de facto, becomes a parental symbol.

Often, the unacknowledged belief is that rewards and recognition are bestowed on the individual rather than being earned by him or her. Consequently, any form of "differentiation" gets equated with "discrimination". In the preliberalization period, most Indian organizations stayed away from performance-linked high differentiation in their reward systems. Postliberalization, the situation has changed considerably, but the anxiety about appearing "non-discriminatory" is fairly common among Indian managers. This is generally dealt with through elaborate quantitative measures of performance and other systems (like moderation and so on) to eliminate subjectivity. More often than not, the focus is on "appearing fair" rather than "being fair".

The other implication of this process is that in competitive situations, jealousy plays a much bigger role than envy. Jealousy is driven more by what we believe the other has received or been bestowed on rather than what the other has achieved. On the other hand, envy leaves some space for recognition of other's superiority in terms of capability or achievement. To that extent, envy can act as a trigger for greater effort and investment in building one's competitiveness. Jealousy can only create grouse and bitterness and, therefore, is more likely to be repressed/suppressed. Keeping all this in view, it is to be expected that competitiveness will be held with some ambivalence in the Indian psyche. Not surprisingly, our respondents find other people as more competitive than themselves.

4. Selflessness, renunciation and faith

The ambivalence towards competitiveness is further reinforced by the emphasis on selflessness and renunciation. These are exalted virtues in most societies but particularly so in Indian culture. This is perhaps because of the threat that personal desires and ambitions pose to the prescribed role imperatives and primacy of the belonging system.

Simultaneously, there is considerable emphasis on fulfilling one's worldly responsibilities. In this respect, the culture does not differentiate between the "householder" and the "ascetic". Most Indian theologies do not promise any great rewards in the afterlife for leading a virtuous life. Instead, freedom from desire is held as the ultimate goal. Consequently, engagement with life and role performance without any "contamination" from personal desires, passions and ambitions is regarded as the most exalted state. In this state, even "aggression" against which there is a strong cultural taboo becomes acceptable. Thus, in many parts of India, the saint soldier has a very special place and to suffer is considered an act of courage and valor.

In such a scenario, it is not easy for any individual to acknowledge own needs, aspirations and ambitions. USD is least identified with (SC) and least valued (SI) by our respondents. However, it figures quite high in their perception of OP. It seems reasonable to assume that this is a case of projection.

For oneself, the person needs the justification of role imperatives in order to pursue own goals. Most commonly deployed justification is "for the sake of my family". In other words, the individual believes that whatever advancement that he or she seeks must ultimately serve the needs of the system to which he or she belongs. For the Self, one must learn to be contented with whatever little one has. It is another matter that in many cases, this stance may be just a rationalization. Thus, it is not uncommon to find parents (or others in a position of higher power) impose their own wishes, desires, needs and so on onto their children with the belief that the same is being done for the betterment of their child. The unintended consequence of this "selflessness" is that the individual appoints him- or herself as the custodian of other people's interest and thereby imposes his or her own will with complete impunity.

Another unintended consequence is the difficulty in claiming one's space and a direct assertion of one's needs. The unstated wish of the individual is that others/system will be sensitive to his or her needs and will fulfill them without being specifically asked. The wish is accompanied by a faith in cosmic benevolence and strong belief that in the ultimate analysis, virtue is always rewarded. In work settings, this "faith" is often transferred on to one's boss and/ or other persons in positions of power.

Not surprisingly, it is expected of a manager/leader to "look after his/her people", and the notion of a benevolent authoritative leader has a strong pull in the Indian psyche. In most Indian organizations, we hear stories of highly charismatic figures who are hugely revered and deified.

For most Indians, the mental picture of an ideal authority relationship has a strong component of a parent–child relationship, as we saw in case of Ravi. It is generally accompanied by a high degree of filial respect, compliance, nurturance and emotional attachment.

Conflict and hostility in an authority relationship become extremely problematic for both sides. As Sudhir and Katharina Kakar point out,

> [i]n stark contrast to the west where generational conflict is not only expected but also considered necessary for the renewal of a society's institutions and, moreover, is considered (we believe erroneously) to be a universally valid psychological truth; in India it is not the rupture but the stretching of traditional values that become a means for the young person to realize his dreams for life.[15]

Thus, according to them, *"[c]harisma plays an unusually significant role among Indians and is a vital constituent of effective leadership in institutions. In contrast to most people in the West, Indians are generally more prone to revere than admire"*.

This does not mean that there is no resentment/hostility towards authority. It only means that resentment and hostility towards authority figures are often displaced on to softer targets (i.e., people lower in status) and/or expressed through passive/silent sabotage (showing disagreement through noncompliance).

Most important, if the authority figures fail to meet the expectations placed on them, then there is a huge sense of "letdown" that is dealt with through callous disregard of others/systems. What the individual seems to be saying is "If the system and people who matter don't care for me, why should I?" Thus, both positive and negatives feelings and actions are attributed to the authority figure. If things are well it is because of the authority figure and if things go bad, it is a failure of the authority figure. The consequence is that reverence and cynicism towards people in positions of power (e.g., political leaders, business tycoons, bureaucrats, spiritual gurus, etc.) happily coexist in India.

The emphasis on selflessness and renunciation also manifests itself in seeking fulfillment through spirituality. An observation made by Dharampal is extremely pertinent in this regard. According to him, the Indian social design offers very little scope for individuality in the temporal space but, simultaneously, propels the individual to seek self-actualization in the spiritual realm. This makes imminent sense if one takes into account the fact that the individual's conduct is largely determined by role imperatives and the accountability to others (particularly members of one's belonging system) is continuously emphasized. Simultaneously, there is a strong message that in the spiritual realm, one is primarily accountable to oneself. A telling example of this is the story of a thief who, in conversation with a wiseman, tries to justify his transgressions as necessary acts committed for the sake of his wife and children. The wiseman reminds him that the spiritual damage caused by these wrongdoings will have to be borne by him and him alone and will not be shared by his family.

Similarly, at the end of the epic *Mahabharata*, Yudhishthira tells his wife and younger brothers that this last journey will have to be undertaken by everyone by himself and herself. For those who believe in the theory of reincarnation, there is a strong belief that one's place in the "next birth" will be determined by one's deeds in this birth. Overall, the message is loud and clear: as a social being, you are essentially a part of the system you belong to and hence accountable to it, *but* as a spiritual being you are accountable only to yourself and have to bear the consequences of your choices and actions by yourself.

This split between the "social self" and the "spiritual self" has significant implications for how "maturity" is configured in the Indian psyche. Our hypothesis is that for most Indians, the picture of a mature individual is one who engages with life without getting entangled into it, who behaves in a role-appropriate fashion, who takes the ups and downs of life in a stoic manner, who cares about people but is emotionally self-sufficient, who is strong and focused but not in your face and who is sensitive but not emotionally volatile and who seeks self-actualization primarily in the spiritual space. On one hand, this helps the individual to be resilient and take things in his or her stride, on the other hand, the pressure of living up to this image (or at least appearing to) not merely takes a huge toll on the spontaneity of the individual but also leaves him or her with tremendous fragility. Often the situation is akin to someone who is desperately trying to appear calm even when sitting on top of a volcano.

Related to this "surface equanimity" is the strong cultural taboo on aggression. An acceptance and the pursuit of one's own agenda enable the individual to assert directly, act decisively and aggress on the environment, if required. In case of Indian psyche, these abilities remain underdeveloped. The flip side is the fear of being aggressed on. Thus, if anyone is seen as assertive or aggressive, he or she is either lionized as heroic or feared as demonic. Overall, it becomes difficult for the individual to handle aggression both in oneself and in others. It is not uncommon to find a handful of ruffians holding large collectives to ransom. Often the aggression does not even have to be of a crude variety – a persistent, unreasonable demand can also be quite effective.

One of us had once asked a CEO why he had agreed to a patently unreasonable demand from one of his direct reports. His reply was quite telling: "I couldn't take the constant pestering for such a small matter". Invariably the transgressions are justified as a small matter, and the individual puts tremendous pressure on Self and others to somehow adjust and turn a blind eye to the transgression.

Swalpa Adjust Madi (a phrase often heard in Bengaluru that means "please adjust a little bit") is not only confined to crowded busses and congested traffic but is also a part of the plush corporate offices of multinational organizations. It is not just reflective of our "adaptability" but also of our need to diffuse potential hostility.

Another typically used excuse for escaping direct confrontation is "I did not want to hurt the other person". The CEO whose example was given earlier is not the only one who withheld what he actually thought and felt even in a relatively higher power position. Many Indian bosses tend to either withhold or sugarcoat their negative evaluations from their subordinates. Part of the reluctance stems from their concern for the feelings of the other person, partly from their need to preserve their relationship, but a significant part stems from the need to protect themselves from potential hostility that they may have to face.

This aversion to direct confrontation pushes many Indian managers into their respective silos. The principle of peaceful coexistence gets translated into keeping a safe distance from each other. Thus, collaboration gets equated to amiability. We recall once some of us had been invited by a CEO to enhance collaboration in his team. When we talked to his team members, we found that the CEO's concern was not shared by them because they believed that they had excellent collaboration among them. From their point of view, they were not fighting with each other, were not getting in each other's way and had very friendly and amiable relationships. It was not easy for them to see that the CEO's concern was very different. He wanted them to relate with each other more openly and candidly, wanted them to address their conflicts more directly and actively support each other rather than keep each other at an arm's length.

In absence of direct combat, conflict situations and power struggles are often dealt with through compromise or resorting to manipulation and external intervention. Also, the aggressive impulses tend to be discharged in safe settings (with people from whom there is no fear of backlash) or insidious expression like sarcasm and malicious gossip.

5. Androgyny and associated ambiguities

Indian attitude towards women was poignantly captured by late Sahir Ludhianwi in the lyric:[16]

> Nari ko is desh ne devi keh kar dasi jana hai jis ko kuch adhikar na ho woh ghar ki rani mana hai
> (In this country woman is called a goddess but treated like a slave, she is the queen of the house but has no rights)

It is tempting to treat this simultaneity of deification and oppression as yet another case of Indian hypocrisy, but the issue may be more complex. Our hypothesis is that this inconsistency is a reflection of the Indian ambivalence towards its androgynous orientation. In order to explore this, it would be useful to make a distinction between patriarchy and patricentricity.

Patriarchy refers essentially to the balance of power in the relationship between the two genders. Thus, preference for a male child, subjugation of women and treating them as property or weaker and, hence, in need of protection and so on are signs of patriarchy.

On the other hand, *patricentricity* refers to a value system and perspective that is primarily governed by our masculine side. Masculinity and femininity are generic principles applicable to both genders and integral to all human beings. However, the relative emphasis varies from person to person. Similarly, cultures vary in the relative emphasis that they place on the two principles. Thus, a patricentric culture lays greater emphasis on masculine orientation and is characterized by features such as purposefulness, goal-directed activity, autonomy, agency, context-free rules, clear boundaries and the like. On the other hand, a matricentric culture places greater emphasis on feminine orientation and is characterized by features such as celebration of life, emphasis on relationships, spontaneous expression, context-specificity, inclusivity, care and compassion, unconditional acceptance of Self and others and so on.

The complexity in the Indian situation arises from the fact that while the social design is based on patriarchy, the cultural ideal is more androgynous than masculine. While men/boys may enjoy a higher social status, there is no clear preference for masculinity per se. In most parts of the country, the notion of an *Ardhanarishwar* (integration of male and female) has a clear edge over a macho alpha male as a cultural ideal.

Sudhir and Kathrina Kakar (2009) have made an interesting observation in respect of gender representations in Indian sculpture as compared to Greek and Roman sculpture:

> This becomes clearer if one thinks of Greek and Roman sculpture which, we believe, has greatly influenced Western gender representations. Here, male gods are represented by hard muscled bodies and chests without any fat. One only needs to compare Greek and Roman statuary with the sculpted representations of Hindu gods, or the Buddha, where the bodies are softer, suppler and, in their hint of breasts, nearer to the female form.

There is an old story of a king who was 'cursed' to become a woman for a certain length of time. However, at the end of the stipulated period, the king chooses to remain a woman as he discovers that being a woman is a lot more enriching, meaningful and satisfying than being a man.

The story can be understood in various ways. At one level, it reinforces the belief of some psychoanalysts that deep down, every man carries a wish to be a woman. While this wish may be quite universal in nature, it appears that it is more pronounced in India.

In a letter to Sigmund Freud, Girindrasekhar Bose,[17] the founder and first president of Indian Psychoanalytical Society, wrote, "*The desire to be a female is more easily unearthed in Indian male patients than in European*".

Thus, not surprisingly, Indian civilization provides a little more space and legitimacy to this wish. The stronghold of Bhakti movement, where every devotee is supposed to be a woman, is a possible reflection of this.

However, the more interesting part of the story is that what was intended to be 'curse' is experienced as a 'blessing'. The story suggests that being a woman is a bio-existential blessing but becomes a social curse. This perhaps is a significant aspect of the way femininity is held in the Indian context and the "hypocrisy" in the treatment of women referred to in the Sahir lyric.

While women occupy a socially inferior position (a logical outcome of a patriarchal society) there is also an acknowledgment of their inherent Shakti (power and energy) and perhaps an underlying belief in their superiority. Thus, almost all temporal pursuits require worship of a female deity – Laxmi for wealth, prosperity and well-being; Saraswati for knowledge and fine arts; and Durga for strength and power. While these goddesses belong to the Hindu pantheon they also have a civilizational significance. Saraswati Vandana is less of a religious ritual and more an invocation of a certain form of feminine energy.

Thus, it appears reasonable to assume that while Indian social design is based on patriarchy, the cultural ideal is more matricentric or at best, androgynous.

As Ashis Nandy (1983) states,

> This undeniably is a matrifocal culture in which femininity is inextricably linked with Prakriti, or nature, and Prakriti with Leela, or activity. Similarly, the concept of adya shakti, primal or original power, is entirely feminine in India – That is why the deities that preside over those critical sectors of life which one cannot control – are all mother figures.

The acknowledgment of the power of the feminine also brings with it terror and apprehension. Thus, in the Shantiparva of the *Mahabharata*, Bhishma advises Yudhishthira to guard against the insatiable female sexuality whereby every man becomes a potential sexual object for a woman (contrary to the sociocultural coding wherein every woman is a sexual object for a man).

Sexuality can also be seen as 'zest for life' and, hence, controlling the 'zest for life' and ensuring that it does not become disruptive and destructive to the social order become a major preoccupation of Indianness.

Perhaps these issues are of concern in all civilizations, but each handles them differently. The Indian way has been to sanitize femininity. Thus, Sati (the faithful wife) and the Mother hold the center stage in Indian femininity. The emphasis is on the nourishing, loving and domesticated side of femininity and glorification of selflessness and complete commitment to the context. It has virtually no space for feminine desires, appetites, lust and wildness. Any woman demonstrating any of these is regarded as an automatic disgrace to womanhood and is treated as a whore. Furthermore, the idea that a woman's Shakti (power) is contingent on her adherence to this frame of sanitized femininity is continuously reinforced through stories, myths, films and popular TV serials.

Simultaneously, there is an uneasy relationship with masculinity. On one hand, since maleness is essentially treated as a social privilege and of no great consequence in the larger scheme of things (the cosmic order being determined by the feminine principle), the Indian notion of masculinity is largely confined to its regulatory side (both for Self and others). The dynamic side of the masculine principle receives much less attention. In fact, Nandy has gone as far as to suggest that several features which are normally considered masculine (e.g., aggression, achievement, control, competition and power) were traditionally associated with femininity in India.

Thus, the segregation of maleness and femaleness are much more ambiguous in the Indian psyche as compared to some other cultures. Our hypothesis is that this psychic ambiguity is compensated by over codification of roles and behavioral norms, particularly for women. Thus, how a woman should dress, speak and the like become major issues of concern, and any deviation from the established norms is seen as a threat to the patriarchal order and dealt with accordingly. We believe that most violence against women in India stems from the need to "put her in her place" and to continually remind her of her "lower social status". The real fear is that "all hell will break loose" if a woman was to deploy her "Shakti" unshackled by the established social order.

The psychic ambiguity not only manifests itself in the area of "man–woman" relationship but also plays a significant role in how the masculine and feminine principles are configured within a person, which, in turn, has significant implications. The following are some:

1   Based upon Carl Jung's theory of the masculine and feminine principles, the later Jungians (like Erich Neumann and Gareth Hill) identified the elementary (or static) and transformative (or dynamic) aspects of these two principles creating a two by two schema.[18] The dynamic masculine pertains to that part of us that says, "I am because I am potent". In its positive form, it enables us to act upon the world and gain mastery over our environment. In its negative form, it leads to insensitivity, violence and destruction.

The static masculine pertains to that part of ourselves that says, "I am because I can think and discern". It manifests itself through regulation, boundary management, self-discipline, rigidity and righteousness. In the EUM frame, the Universe that has the maximum resonance with static masculine is URB, which is also the most identified with by our respondents.

This is quite understandable. Given the various features of Indian identity (like emphasis on selflessness, primacy of belonging, association of hierarchy with purity/pollution, etc.) the features of static masculine are much easier to integrate than those of dynamic masculine. In fact, according to Ashis Nandy, in the Indian context, the dynamic masculine features are treated primarily as feminine part of the cosmos. Thus, he states, "[i]n the traditional concept of manliness, the Brahmin in his cerebral, self-denying asceticism was the traditional masculine counterpoint to the more violent, 'virile', active Kshatriya, the later representing – however odd this may seem to modern consciousness- the feminine principle in the cosmos".

This overidentification with the static masculine and the uneasy relationship with dynamic masculine manifests themselves in various ways, such as in having difficulty in owning up own needs, desires and ambitions; needing systemic legitimacy to assert oneself, displacement of aggression on safe targets and so on, many of which have already been mentioned earlier. Most important, it makes it very difficult for the individual to exercise "agency" in a responsible manner.

The individual either gives up all agency or acts in utter disregard for the consequences. In our experience, the only significant exception to this phenomenon is when the person is operating from the psychological role of being a "Son". This "son-hood" is not necessarily confined to one's own family or parents. It can easily be extended to one's boss, leader, organization or any other system of belonging.

In our collective experience of working with thousands of people, we have found that "Son-hood" plays a very important role in identity formation. Rama (the loyal, obedient carrier of heritage) is, of course, the cultural ideal, but there are several variants of the son role (the prodigal son, the defiant son, the neglected son, the sacrificing son, the proxy son and so on) In many ways, the way the individual sees his son-hood becomes a significant determinant of identity.

Even among women, we find that it becomes much easier for them to operate from dynamic masculinity when they are acting "on behalf" of the system. Simply put, whether it be men or women, the dissolution (or at least a temporary suspension) of ambivalence towards dynamic masculinity requires a strong systemic justification.

2   Just as there are two aspects of the masculine principle, there are two aspects of the feminine principle as well. The static feminine principle operates on unconditional acceptance of Self, context and imperatives of living. It nourishes and sustains life but also entraps in a ritualistic existence. The dynamic feminine, on the other hand, enlivens and transforms. It not only is the source of creativity and zest for life but can also lead to hysteria, moodiness, despair, addiction and destruction.

Given the preoccupation with sanitized femininity and fears associated with its destructive potential, the Indian psyche has a very uneasy relationship with the dynamic aspect of the feminine principle. This manifest itself not just in man–woman relationships but also in the individual's relatedness with his or her own intensity and spontaneity. Thus, two adjectives that have the greatest resonance with the dynamic feminine principle (*Emotional* and *Uninhibited*) are neither identified with nor valued by our respondents.

This orientation, on one hand, enables the individual to accept the role demands and contextual imperatives with a reasonable degree of equanimity; it also limits the transformative potential, particularly of a kind which entails destruction and upsetting the apple cart. Thus, often Indian ingenuity finds expression in coping situations (Jugaad) rather than in transformative situations.

Another unintended consequence of distancing from the dynamic femininity is that the individual starts seeking "excitement" vicariously. We suspect that the two major Indian passions, Bollywood and cricket, have much to do with this "stimulus hunger" and need for drama. In daily living, this search for excitement manifests through gossip and involvement in issues of other people that, in many cultures, may be considered as interference into personal domain.

3   The androgynous/feminine leaning has also been a source of considerable stress in the Indian psyche. Indians have often been referred to as "effeminate" in a derogatory sort of way. It has

also created a self-doubt: Is our feminine/androgynous leaning a choice/conviction, or is it a mere cover-up for our cowardice? As with all such questions, chances are that both are equally true. While androgyny/feminine leaning may have provided a convenient escape route from facing up to one's fears and anxieties, there is also likely to be a civilizational preference for it. However, it becomes extremely difficult to grace this preference if it is experienced as a liability. This phenomenon is extremely pronounced amongst women all over the world. Increasing they are being compelled to distance themselves from femininity (particularly of the static variety) because of the experience of having suffered on account of it.

We suspect something similar is happening to the Indian psyche. Not merely is there the historical baggage of external invasions/foreign rule, but also there are the current imperatives of living in the present-day world, where dynamic masculinity rules the roost. This is particularly applicable to the section of Indians who have greater exposure to institutions (like the corporate world), which are designed primarily on dynamic masculine principle.

Consequently, what to do with their civilization preference for androgyny/femininity in a dynamic masculine world remains a difficult question for many Indians.

6. Two faces of Indianness

It is easy to see that the features described earlier are interrelated and reinforce each other. Thus, preoccupation with hierarchy is reinforced by both context sensitivity and primacy of belonging system. Similarly, emphasis on selflessness is related to primacy of belonging system, and reverence towards authority figures makes it easy for the individual to have faith in the intrinsic benevolence and fairness of the system. The strong emphasis on static masculine and distancing from dynamic feminine are closely related to preoccupation with roles and hierarchy as well as to difficulties with spontaneous expression and intensity. Overall the different features hang together and make a fairly cogent picture.

However, there are two sides to this broad picture of Indianness. The first side is of a gentle, amiable, open, inclusive person who has strong roots in his or her system of belonging. The person wishes to fulfill role obligations with honor and dignity and live in harmony with others and the environment. Everything, including oneself, is regarded as minuscule part of the divine/cosmic wholeness. The individual is strongly anchored in faith and extremely resilient in dealing with ups and downs of life with equanimity. The operative principle for the person is to act in accordance with Dharma and accept the consequences.

The second picture is of a "frog in the well" who is too timid to venture out and has little power to deal with adverse forces. The person who is caught with shame and self-doubt mistrusts everyone but meekly accepts whatever is thrown at him or her. The person runs from direct confrontation and relies primarily on connivance to get along and get ahead in life. While this person easily surrenders in front of people who are more powerful, he or she does not hesitate to oppress all those who are less than him or her.

Which of these is the "real Indian"? It is tempting to treat the first picture as real Indianness and the second as a mere distortion. On the other hand, one can regard the second picture as real Indianness and the first as a romantic fantasy. Perhaps the reality is that the two pictures are intimately connected and merely constitute two sides of the same coin. Thus, it is not surprising that most of the popular Indian television serials are based on this split. Invariably, the main protagonist conforms to the first picture and his or her detractors to the second.

This split is also reflected in our EUM data. The SC scores come quite close to the first picture whereas the OP scores paint the second picture. In other words, our respondents identify with the first picture and project the second picture on to others. Simply put, what they seem to be saying is "Most other people (presumably Indians) are of the second variety, and hence, I am forced to become like them, though my personal inclination is towards the first picture".

The impact of this split can also be seen in the Ravi–Hema case described in the previous chapter. Presumably, Ravi's perception of himself would be along the lines of the first picture, but Hema is more likely to see the second picture in him. While it would be helpful if Hema could see Ravi the way he sees himself, but that by itself would not be sufficient. From Hema's point of view, even the first picture falls short of her expectations and requirements.

Hema's expectations and requirements are based on what she sees as the imperatives of living in the present-day world. Individualistic, democratic, market-driven societies are built on the assumption that the responsible pursuit of self-interest is the key to collective well-being and, thus, have a clear tilt towards the right side of the spiral (USD and UPA) This is even more applicable to the corporate world which is largely built around the UPA/Network philosophy. This may be an overly simplistic view of the human situation, but it cannot be disregarded either. No matter what ideology one subscribes to, there is no getting away from the importance of the pursuit of responsible self-interest. In this respect, both pictures of Indianness fall short. In the first picture, the individual remains caught with "self-denial" and, hence, finds it difficult to own up and pursue own needs/desires/goals. In the second picture, the individual is so self-absorbed that he or she loses sight of the responsibility towards the context. In either case, the pursuit of self-interest with responsibility becomes difficult.

Similarly, Hema's perception of herself is likely to be aligned with the SI picture drawn by our respondents: a person primarily driven by UPA within the overall URB frame but who sees little relevance for UMI in the corporate world. Here again, Ravi's perception of Hema would be aligned to the OP picture: as someone who is too self-centered and ambitious to care for either humanistic considerations or values and principles. Even if Ravi could see Hema, the way she sees herself, he would still find it difficult to come to terms with her basic perspective.

The difficulties between Hema and Ravi are not merely of distorted perceptions but also of different perspectives. These differences arise from their respective engagements with their civilizational predispositions. Ravi finds it difficult to release himself from their captivity whereas Hema is unable to grace them and integrate them with her professional life. So long as they remain entrenched in these positions, it will be very difficult for them to see the necessity to co-hold their seemingly opposite perspectives.

The essential question is whether the perspectives of Hema and Ravi can be meaningfully co-held. In order to engage with this question, we need to explore how these perspectives play out in managerial/leadership behaviors and orientations.

Notes

1 Morris, G. H. (1967). *Mind, Self, and Society from the Standpoint of a Social Behaviorist*. Chicago: University of Chicago Press.
2 Garg, P. (1989). *Cultural Identities – Their Implications for Patterns of Leadership in Indian Organizations*. Indian Society for Individual and Social development compilation. p. 3.-

3 Ramanujam, A. K. (1989). Is there an Indian way of thinking? An informal essay. *Contributions to Indian Sociology*, 23(1).

4 Hegel, G. W. (1902). *Lectures on the Philosophy of History* (J. Sibree, Trans.). London: George Bell and Sons.

5 Ashrama Dharma recognizes four ashramas or stages in the life of a human being. They are *brahmacharya* (stage of studentship), *grihasta* (the stage of a householder), *vanaprastha* (stage of a forest dweller) and *sanyasa* (stage of renunciation). The central belief is that notion of dharma (righteous conduct) is different for each ashrama, that is, stage of life.

6 *Swadharma* means our true nature, the way we are made in terms of our internal instincts and attributes. Swadharma thus makes everyone of us unique in our own way. Swadharma is the way of self and acting in accordance with one's own true nature.

7 *Appadharma* is often explained as the dharma of abnormal times, for it sanctions any means to desired end. Under perilous circumstances, the normal rules of righteous conduct do not apply.

8 A *raga* is an array of melodic structures with musical motifs, considered in the Indian tradition to have the ability to "color the mind" and affect the emotions of the audience. It has no direct translation to concepts in the classical European music tradition. Each *raga* consists of at least five notes, and each *raga* provides the musician with a musical framework. Each *raga* has an emotional significance and symbolic associations such as with season, time and mood.

9 Richard Allan Shweder (b. 1945) is an American cultural anthropologist. He is currently Harold H. Swift Distinguished Service Professor of Human Development in the Department of Comparative Human Development at the University of Chicago. He is the author of *Thinking Through Cultures: Expeditions in Cultural Psychology* (1991) and *Why Do Men Barbecue? Recipes for Cultural Psychology* (2003). Shweder's main fieldwork outside the United States has been in the temple town of Bhubaneswar in the state of Odisha, India. Among other topics, his fieldwork in India has looked at cross-cultural concepts of the person, self, emotions and moral reasoning. He has advocated forms of cultural pluralism while being mindful of the practical and ethical difficulties certain kinds of pluralism entail.

10 Alan Roland, PhD, is a psychoanalyst, author, artist and playwright/librettist. He has made seminal contributions in the area of cross-cultural psychology with Asians and Asian Americans, having written three books on the subject, including *In Search of Self in India and Japan: Towards a Cross-Cultural Psychology* (1988), *Cultural Pluralism and Psychoanalysis: The Asian and North American Experience* (1996) and *Journeys to Foreign Selves: The Asian and North American Experience*. (2011)

11 Nandy, A. (1983). *The Intimate Enemy: Loss and Recovery of Self under Colonialism*. Oxford: Oxford University Press.

12 Thomas Babington Macaulay played a major role in introducing English and Western concepts to education in India, publishing his argument on the subject in the *Macaulay Minute*, published in 1835. He supported the replacement of Persian by English as the official

language, the use of English as the medium of instruction in all schools, and the training of English-speaking Indians as teachers. In his view, Macaulay divided the world into civilized nations and barbarism, with Britain representing the high point of civilization. In his *Minute on Indian Education* of February 1835, he asserted, "*It is, I believe, no exaggeration to say that all the historical information which has been collected from all the books written in the Sanskrit language is less valuable than what may be found in the paltriest abridgement used at preparatory schools in England*". In Indian culture, the term *Macaulay's Children* is sometimes used to refer to people born of Indian ancestry who adopt Western culture as a lifestyle or display attitudes influenced by colonization.

13 *Bombay* by Mani Ratnam is a 1995 Indian Tamil-language Indian romantic drama film that is centered on events that occurred particularly during the period of December 1992 to January 1993 in India and the controversy surrounding the Babri Masjid in Ayodhya and its subsequent demolition on December 6, 1992. This demolition increased religious tensions in the city of Bombay (now Mumbai) that led to the Bombay Riots. It is the second in Ratnam's trilogy of films that depict human relationships against a background of Indian politics, including *Roja* (1992) and *Dil Se* (1998)

14 House, R. J. et al. (2004). *Leadership Culture and Organisations: The GLOBE Study of 62 Societies*. Thousand Oaks, CA: Sage Publications.

15 Kakar, S. K. (2009). *The Indians: Portrait of a People*. Penguin Books.

16 Ludhianvi, S. (Writer) and Kale, K. N. (Director). (1959). *Didi* [Motion Picture].

17 Girindrasekhar Bose (January 30, 1887–June 3, 1953) was an early 20th-century South Asian psychoanalyst and the first president (1922–1953) of the Indian Psychoanalytic Society. Bose carried on a 20-year dialog with Sigmund Freud. Known for disputing the specifics of Freud's Oedipal theory, he has been pointed to by some as an early example of non-Western contestations of Western methodologies.

18 Hill, G. (1992). *Masculine and Feminine – The Natural Flow of Opposites in the Psyche*. Shambala Publications.

Chapter 7

Leadership polarities and Indian managers

Engagement with polarities is at the heart of leadership

Irrespective of whether we look at leadership as a collective process or individual behavior, engagement with seemingly opposite pulls remains an integral part of it. It is reasonably well accepted both by academicians and by practitioners that there are no absolutes in leadership.

Efficacy of leadership behavior/process is contingent on several factors – the dispositions of the people concerned and demands of the situation being the most important. However, in every situation, there are multiple pulls, and in every person, there are multiple dispositions. Many of these multiple forces often conflict with each other, and how the consequent tensions are engaged with has a significant impact on the performance, the well-being and future of the system. Thus, negotiating these apparently opposing forces (polarities) and enabling the system to take a stance become the most important leadership functions.

While each participating stakeholder/leader tries to balance/co-hold these polarities in accordance with the demands of the situation, his or her own disposition also plays a significant role in this process. Thus, in a situation where "task demands" may conflict with "concern for people", some manager or stakeholder/leaders may lean towards the former whereas some others may have a distinct preference for the latter. Similarly, some leaders may tend to take a "long-term" perspective while some others may be governed by immediate goals.

The number of polarities faced by leaders is infinite and no list can possibly cover all of them. In the EUM framework, we focus on four polarities, and in our understanding/experience, these four polarities cover/subsume most dilemmas faced by leaders. What follows is

a   a brief description of these polarities, and
b   insights about how they are engaged with by Indian managers based upon EUM data and our collective experience.

1. Preservation versus Transformation

Every living system (including human beings, groups, teams, families, organizations, etc.) works towards preserving its integrity/ wholeness. The notion of integrity and wholeness is defined by the context in the past, and in order to maintain its continuity, the system seeks to perpetuate the very same regardless of the emergent forces within and outside it.

Simultaneously (and paradoxically enough) every system strives to evolve and transform itself. The need for transformation may stem from the demands of adapting to a dynamic environment and/ or to fulfill its own inherent potential.

No system can escape this paradoxical duality: in order to survive, it must evolve, and in order to evolve, it must first survive.

Leaders in their attempt to co-hold this polarity tend to lean towards one side or another.

Leaders who lean towards the preservation side tend to place a premium on continuity, tradition and established ways of the system. They view the system as a collation of different parts and focus on ensuring that each part plays its role effectively and works in tandem with other parts.

Often when the system is formed or designed, the people across the system share the same picture; however, with time, this shared picture of the system gets reduced to a fragmented or myopic lens – soon comes a time, when each subsystem gets focused on its own fragmented view and its preservation. Consequently, the task of the leaders becomes one of ensuring that these fragments can coexist in a reasonably coherent manner.

Perforce, they have to place a high emphasis on smooth interfaces, diffusing conflicts and/or working towards acceptable compromises. Such leaders tend to forge a stable relationship with the environment and emphasize loyalty in their relationships with multiple stakeholders. They prefer gradual incremental movement to discontinuous change and are reasonably comfortable in playing supportive roles.

A typical statement about Self and Others by a preservation-centric leader is likely to read as shown in Box 7.1.

Box 7.1   Preservation-centric

I resist temptations, fads and other external developments and worry about their influence on my people. I would not wish them to go astray. I have diligently carried forward the legacy of my revered mentor. I often cite my own growth to illustrate that tenure, duty and loyalty are rewarding. I believe past ways have merit and must not be cast aside without review. Many of the people who work for me are like 'family', and the fabric of togetherness is a great source of pride, strength and solace.

In the EUM framework, we have discovered that these leaders have a greater inclination towards UBP and URB and are generally averse towards USD – the latter Universe is seen as disruptive. These leaders are very effective in stable environments and in dealing with people who have a high need for clarity/predictability and are not very high on aggression and ambition. Contexts, which have clear boundaries, role definitions and structural authority, bring out the best in these leaders. However, they may experience some difficulty in turbulent environments and/or dealing with people who are assertive and ambitious.

Leaders who lean towards transformation engage with the dynamicity of the environment and the unrealized potential of the system. They focus on envisioning a future state and propel the system towards actualizing this vision. They tend to look at chaos and conflict as a resource and work towards harnessing its creative potential. They are extremely effective in situations that require proactive engagement, provided they have sufficient elbow room to experiment and explore.

While they work well with people who are energetic and ambitious, they run the risk of becoming insensitive to other people's need for order and stability.

A typical statement about Self and Others by a transformation-centric leader is likely to read as shown in Box 7.2.

Box 7.2 Transformation -centric

I tend to be restless and impatient with doing the same things over and over and staying with the tried-and-tested ways. I scout for opportunities to improve upon what exists. I am not sentimental or nostalgic about the past and tend to be future focused. In creating the future of my dreams, I actively seek out people who are willing to join in and forge alliances. I invest in preparedness and prefer to treat setbacks as learning opportunities. I recognize that the world is ever changing and that I must tailor my moves to respond to what is emerging and take risks that improve the probability of my success.

In the EUM framework, these leaders are more inclined towards UPA, USD and UDS and are generally uncomfortable with UBP features both in themselves and in other people.

Table 7.1 illustrates the difference between preservation-centric and transformation-centric leadership.

Table 7.1 Preservation versus transformation

Dimension	Preservation-centric	Transformation-centric
Orientation towards Universes	• Greater affinity towards UBP and URB and aversion towards USD	• Greater affinity towards USD, UPA and UDS and aversion towards UBP
Purpose	• Leaders would emphasize the need for stability, balance, fairness and structures that enhance the preservation of systems.	• Leaders would emphasize on disruption, conflict, experimentation and learning processes to evoke transformation of the system.
Source of Energy	• Leaders would get energized by the knowns, the oughts and shoulds, the traditions, and the legacies.	• Leaders would get energized by unfulfilled potential, dissatisfaction, disruption and moving into the unknown.

(Continued)

Table 7.1 (Continued)

Dimension	Preservation-centric	Transformation-centric
Nature of Relationships	• Leaders would emphasize on smooth interfaces, communal processes, role-based relationships – valuing the focus on adjustment–accommodation–compliance processes.	• Leaders would emphasize on individualism, agency and purposive relationships. They would value passion, confrontation, courage and risk taking.
Basis of Decision Making	• Leaders would make decisions on the basis of legacies, prevailing Dharma, and sustaining the institutional values.	• Leaders would make decisions based on determinism, rationality, purpose and movement beyond the known.

The Indian experience: what our data reveals

The scores of Indian managers on the dimensions of preservation and transformation are summarized in Table 7.2.

Table 7.2 Orientation of Indian managers in the first polarity

Dimension	SC	SI	OP
Preservation	47.23	36.76	41.54
Transformation	44.98	49.80	52.68

Note: Each score is on a 0–100 scale.

- As can be seen from this data, our respondents identify with both dimensions to a moderate extent, and their SC scores are fairly balanced, with a slight tilt towards the preservation side.
- The same pattern is shown with respect to the relative scores as compared to OP. Their beliefs seem to be that other people lean more towards transformation than they do, whereas they are more concerned with preservation.
- However, when it comes to looking at SI, the balance shifts towards transformation. Significantly, the drop from SC to SI in case of preservation (more than 10 points) is much more than the increase in transformation scores (less than 5 points).

This perhaps indicates some unease with the present situation but hesitation to act.

- Thus, blending continuity with change is likely to be the preferred way for Indian managers. Change efforts that create too much disruption in the established ways and that are seen as upsetting the apple cart are likely to be met with resistance.
- However, given the low USD orientation in the Indian psyche, this resistance may remain more passively than actively expressed. In our experience, we have often found that this passive resistance is often ignored or brushed aside. The consequence is that change agenda is only superficially assimilated, and people find ingenious ways of merrily carrying on with their accustomed ways. Silent sabotage and public agreement but private disagreements, among other behaviors, exemplify this passive resistance towards many transformational initiatives.
- The other significant factor pertains to the nature of transformation energy. It is important to note that for both UPA and USD (the two main Universes which feed the transformation energy), the OP scores are higher than the SC scores. This suggests that the individual carries a feeling that others are moving faster than he or she is and is thus likely to be operating more from the *fear of being left behind* rather than from a real desire to fulfill one's own potential. Furthermore, a low USD orientation coupled with a reasonably high UPA orientation suggests a degree of proxy-hood, that is, a state where the individual is mobilized by goals given to him or her rather than by his or her own dreams and desires.
- Overall, the picture seems to be of a person who wishes to co-hold preservation with transformation but who is somewhat reluctant to envision either for oneself or for the system. Simultaneously, the person is experiencing some restlessness and wishes to place more emphasis on transformation. In this scenario, it would be easier for the person to energize him- or herself if clear goal/directions are provided to him or her rather than the person being expected to self-authorize.

2. Meritocracy versus Humanism

Another significant source of tension is the competing pull between demands of meritocracy and the need for humanistic values.

Every system has a *primary task*, which is the raison d'être for its existence – this is equally applicable to affiliative systems like family. Consequently, task performance and contribution towards fulfillment of this primary task have to be treated as the guiding principle in its governance. In this sense, every individual member can be seen as a robotic/instrumental entity with some capabilities, skills, competencies and knowledge that get deployed to add some value to the system.

However, any system is also a *human community* that exists for itself and, hence, finds it necessary to foster its own well-being. This is equally true of all its constituents also. These constituents are not robotic instruments of purpose but living human beings who have their own thoughts, feelings, needs, desires, values, preferences and so on.

These human features can be seen as both an asset and a liability for the primary task. On one hand, these aspects often divert the focus away from performing the task, and on the other hand, the systemic tasks cannot be fulfilled if the members do not bring their innate humanness into the system. Similarly, the individual and collective well-being cannot be sustained if the primary task is not being engaged with.

Thus, the instrumental/performing aspect of the system has an interdependent relationship with its human side. The two cannot exist without each other, and yet the two have an inherent contrary pull. Not surprisingly, the relative emphasis on the task and people dimensions figures prominently in virtually any discourse on leadership theory and practice. While every leader strives to co-hold these competing demands, the leader also has his or her own innate inclination.

People who lean towards the meritocracy side tend to view systems as purposive entities and continually push themselves/others towards higher levels of performance. Their decisions around human beings (including empowering, motivating, learning, rewarding, etc.) are governed by aspects and measures of merit, competence and contribution, and they encourage a spirit of healthy competition among their people.

They find it easy to express criticism and are generally willing to take hard decisions, if necessary. They are willing to invest in learning and development both for themselves and others, provided they see it as relevant for the task needs. They generally tend to stay away from forging emotional links with people, and their relationships are marked by either high power distance or functionality. They are often held with considerable respect, particularly by those who have a high need for achievement and learning. They may experience difficulties with people who need empathy and emotional support and/or who are differentially talented.

A typical statement about Self and Others by a meritocracy-centric leader is likely to read as shown in Box 7.3.

Box 7.3 Meritocracy-centric

I believe that current form is more important than past records. All my people work to stay sharp and capable, focused and competitive. People who grow around me are those who are willing to challenge their previous best on an ongoing basis. I set high standards for myself and others. I create a context where striving is important, but results beget rewards. I ensure that essential systems are in place so that the challenges are about value addition rather than heroic crisis management. It helps when people get along, but I make it clear that plans, tasks and outcomes take precedence over amiability and making allowances for the needs and limitations of people.

In the EUM framework, these leaders have a strong pull towards UPA and at least a moderate degree of comfort with USD and URB.

Leaders who lean towards the humanistic side, view systems as human communities which are governed by feelings, needs, desires and expectations of their people. Consequently, they focus on building healthy ambience, forging intimate relationships and trying to promote goodwill and collaboration. They prefer inclusive and participative decision making and show a high acceptance of diversity. While they are very effective in situations that require sensitive and empathetic engagement across a diverse set of people, they run the risk of underestimating environmental threats and may find it difficult to take hard, decisive and unilateral action.

A typical statement about Self and Others by a humanistic leader is likely to read as shown in Box 7.4.

In the EUM framework, these leaders have a strong affinity towards UMI and at least a moderate degree of comfort with UBP.

Table 7.3 illustrates the differences between meritocratic and humanistic leadership.

The Indian experience: what our data reveal

Box 7.4 Humanism-centric

I frequently ask myself: Do my people feel good coming to work each day? Do they find their work meaningful? Am I paying heed to their feelings, views, opinions and suggestions? Since each person is different and all are not at their peak at any given time, I try to be accommodating of the range of preparedness and limitations, forgiving of shortfalls, and seek to inspire people to a better performance the next time around. I am mindful and attempt to contain the impact of business decisions on people. I try and ensure that decisions regarding placement, rewards and promotions and punitive actions do not compromise respect, dignity and morale.

The scores of Indian managers on these two dimensions are summarized in Table 7.4.

- These data shows that our respondents value meritocracy a lot more than humanism. The SI scores with respect to meritocracy are more than double as compared to humanism (68.64 as compared to 27.16).
- They also see themselves as more meritocratic (58.86) than humanistic (39.75).
- However, the situation changes significantly in respect of how they see themselves in comparison to other people. In their view, other people are even more meritocratic and less humanistic than they are.
- Put together, our respondents seem to be saying, "*I am more humanistic than most other people are, and if I wish to become more meritocratic then it is necessary for me to reduce my humanistic orientation*".
- It appears that these two dimensions are seen by our respondents as antithetical to each other. As stated earlier UPA and UMI (which are the prime movers of this polarity) have the highest negative correlation. This implies an interesting split of the polarity – an "either–or" pattern of choice. Thus, co-creating and sustaining task and sentient systems may create difficulties for the Indian manager.

Table 7.3 Meritocracy versus humanism

Dimension	Humanism-centric	Meritocracy-centric
Orientation towards Universes	• Have a strong affinity towards UMI and a moderate degree of comfort with UBP. May be averse to USD within Self as well as others.	• Have a strong affinity towards UPA and a moderate degree of comfort with USD and URB Universes. May be averse to UBP and UMI
Purpose	• To create and reinforce 'sentient systems' that focus on renewal and replenishment of the system	• To deploy tasks and processes aligned to goals and outputs of the system
Source of energy	• Leaders would get energized by emotions and a need to look at the emotional well-being of all within the system. Dependency, call for nurturing and intimacy would energize the leader.	• Leaders would get energized by goals, purpose and performance – efficiency, creativity and innovation, improvement. Striving for better standards, ideation, action and competency would energize the leader.
Nature of relationships	• *Intimate, empathetic, compassionate, inclusive* are words that would describe the nature of relationships. The leader would endorse nurturance, camaraderie, bonhomie and diversity.	• The nature of relationships would be purposive, collaboration amongst equals and instrumental. The leader would endorse action orientation, challenge when required and reinforce goal-based relationships.
Basis of decision making	• Would be guided by feelings of people, their involvement and collective ownership of the decision	• Would be based on goal accomplishment, results orientation, capabilities and competencies and expediency.

Table 7.4 Orientation of Indian managers in the second polarity

Dimension	SC	SI	OP
Meritocracy	56.86	68.64	63.22
Humanism	39.75	27.16	31.93

Note: Each score is on a 0–100 scale.

- There are, of course, leaders who can exploit the synergy between humanism and meritocracy, but it seems that for a large majority, the two are locked in an adversarial relationship.
- We have come across several managers who experience considerable difficulty in seeing the relevance of UMI/Ecological Universes for the corporate world. Their first reaction often is "Are you talking about NGOs [nongovernmental organizations] and social workers?" In their minds, the features of UMI/Ecological have no place in the corporate world, which should only be governed by UPA/Network philosophy.
- Our hypothesis is that traditionally, this polarity has been managed by strong charismatic leaders. Thus, in many organizations we hear stories about a charismatic figure who was extremely demanding and caring at the same time. Given the primacy of order and continuity in the Indian psyche, it is no surprise that such people create an aura of dependability around them, and it is very easy for the collectives to place almost blind faith in them. Whatever is done by such leaders is automatically considered to be in the best interest of everybody. Such leaders are held as the role models, and people like Ravi aspire to be like them.
- This overreliance on a few individuals makes it very difficult for people to see the co-holding of meritocracy and humanism as a collective endeavor, and it gets assigned to a handful of chosen few.

Another difficulty arises from some of the frozen meanings associated with both meritocracy and humanism. In our experience, humanism is often interpreted in a soft, sentimental sort of way with very little room for authentic encounter and confrontation. One often comes across managers who refrain from giving negative feedback to their subordinates lest they hurt their feelings. Similarly, exercising lateral and upward authority is shunned in the name of respect, concern and host of similar so-called humanistic values. The end result is that humanism gets reduced to mere interface management and a convenient escape from the unpleasant task of engaging with harsh realities.

A striking example of this phenomenon can be found in the engagement surveys conducted by many organizations. We have often found that response to a statement like "I am treated with respect" receives fairly high scores. Simultaneously, statements like "I receive honest and regular feedback" OR "I am consulted on decisions which affect me" receive much lower scores. The disparity raises the obvious question: What does respect mean if it is not accompanied by authenticity and relevant involvement? A reasonable hypothesis would be that all that the respondents are saying is that no one shouts at them or behaves badly with them, but nevertheless, they end up being taken for granted. The underlying indignity and patronization of this process are rarely recognized.

Such superficial interpretations of humanism lead to a situation where authentic engagement is replaced by polite diplomatic interfaces. Not surprisingly, our EUM-O data show a sharp drop for the word *Diplomatic* from OC to OI. However, while our respondents want their organizations to become less diplomatic, for themselves they want to become more *Tactful*, which sees a large jump from SC to SI in EUM-I. Needless to say, this superficial interpretation of humanism adds to the difficulty of co-holding it with demands of meritocracy.

Much the same can be said about meritocracy. Invariably, it is interpreted in terms of "deliverables" and targets and that, too, on a quarter-to-quarter basis. The institutional contribution/damage and the invisible waste that may have got caused in the pursuit of these numbers are rarely taken into account. Not surprisingly, in most organizations, the picture of an effective leader carries many more masculine attributes (assertiveness, analytical ability, ambition, action orientation, etc.) than feminine attributes (caring, compassion, intuitiveness, tolerance, receptivity, etc.). Even competencies that have a direct bearing on the human dimension (e.g., teamwork, interpersonal effectiveness, collaboration, etc.) are interpreted superficially and only in behavioral terms. It is enough for the person to behave "appropriately", and how he or she actually feels is regarded as a personal matter and of no consequence.

Needless to say, such superficial interpretations of both humanism and meritocracy leave very little common ground between them, and it is no surprise that our respondents see them as antithetical to each other.

3. Control versus Empowerment

For a system to maintain its coherence, it is necessary that all its constituents operate in a reasonably predetermined, predictable and consistent manner. Hence, every system needs control mechanisms, which could be personalized supervision/monitoring and/or structural and systemic provisions.

Simultaneously, each subsystem (individual, group, division, etc.) requires a certain degree of autonomy (to act on behalf of itself) and a sense of empowerment (to act on behalf of the larger system) in order to meet the demands of a dynamic environment, as well as to actualize its own potential. The tension between the need for control and need for empowerment is engaged both through *structure* (centralization vs. decentralization, delegation of powers, etc.) and through *managerial orientation* of individual leaders who differ in the relative emphasis they place on these two sides.

Leaders, who lean towards the control side, tend to view the system as a collation of different parts with each having its specific agenda. These specific agendas sometimes converge and sometimes diverge; hence, these leaders focus on monitoring the functioning of each part, ensure that they have a firm grip on what is going on and thereby ensure that the different parts are relating to each other in an optimal manner. They put emphasis on procedures, outputs, efficiencies and error-proofing. They are comfortable with taking unilateral decisions and generally disseminate information on the "need-to-know" basis. They prefer homogeneity and work towards nipping conflicts in the bud or settling them quickly. The control side reinforces a mechanistic orientation to systems and subsystems and encourages compliance.

Such leaders are extremely effective in dealing with situations that need single-point anchorage; quick, decisive action; and engagement with people who need guidance/pushing. They may face difficulty in situations that have multiple sources of power and influence and/or people who have a high need for autonomy.

A typical statement about Self and Others by a control-centric leader is likely to read as shown in Box 7.5.

Box 7.5 Control-centric

I tend to ensure that things do not go out of hand and reach a point where it may be hard to pull back the reins and restore them to an even keel. I get personally involved wherever possible as it is important that people I work with understand exactly what I have in mind and want of them. I like to keep a close eye on things and instruct people on the details that I am afraid may be overlooked. I have close and faithful confidantes and stringent reporting requirements that help me to be on top of a situation. I like being prepared for eventualities rather than suffer rude surprises at a late stage. I would like people to know who is in charge, and I use every opportunity to underline that.

In the EUM framework, these leaders have a strong inclination towards USD and URB with low scores for UDS. People with higher USD prefer personalized control whereas people with higher URB prefer structural mechanisms. A repressed or denied lens of UDS enables the reduction of complexity and plurality within the system – making it easier for control. Low UDS scores reinforce the fantasy that managers cannot just control but also solve all problems either through structure (URB) or through personal power (USD).

People who lean towards the empowerment side tend to view the system as an organic whole and work towards enhancing its ability to self-regulate and self-authorize. They prefer to facilitate rather than direct and lead from the front. Consequently, they tend to encourage differences, create spaces for dialog and try to build consensus in their decision-making process. They are open and transparent and share information not just on a need-to-know basis but also to create an ambience of greater involvement.

Such leaders are most effective in situations that require co-holding/networking and dealing with people who are self-motivated and willing to invest in their development. They may experience difficulties in situations that require quick/unilateral action and in dealing with people who need clear directions and pushing.

A typical statement about Self and Others by an empowerment-centric leader is likely to read as shown in Box 7.6.

Box 7.6 Empowerment-centric

I feel secure in the knowledge that I have self-motivated and competent people working with me. I recognize that I cannot be in many places and juggling too many tasks at the same time, and I am comfortable depending on others to take charge of different areas. I have often felt that my people must experience space and opportunities to initiate, perform, try things and even fail. I trust my people take action based on available knowledge and their best judgment, engage among themselves to find answers to questions and include me where necessary. My success depends on others.

In the EUM framework, such leaders lean towards UPA, UMI and UDS.

Table 7.5 summarizes the key aspects of control and empowerment.

The Indian experience: what our data reveal

The scores of Indian managers on these two dimensions are summarized in Table 7.6.

- Our data suggest that the Indian managers place moderate and equal emphasis on both dimensions of this polarity. However, they wish to become a little less controlling and a little more empowering.
- Interestingly, they believe that other people are both more controlling and empowering than themselves, though the controlling score is higher than the empowering score for other people. This suggests an uneasy relationship with both sides of this polarity.
- If we look at the Universe scores for URB and USD, we find that in case of URB, the SC scores are significantly higher in SC than OP whereas in case of USD, the scores in OP are significantly higher than the SC scores.
- Put together, what our respondents seem to be saying, "I like to adhere to systemic discipline and operate within the prescribed rules, but others seem to have scant respect for rules and systems and are going by their own self-centered agenda".

Table 7.5 Control- versus empowerment

Dimension	Control-centric	Empowerment-centric
Tilt towards Universes	• Have a strong affinity towards USD and URB. May be averse towards UDS	• Have a strong affinity towards UMI, and at least moderate level of comfort with UPA and UDS. May be averse to USD.
Purpose	• Eliminating deviance and ensuring consistent delivery	• Enhancing the ability of the system to self-regulate and for people to initiate and self-authorize
Source of energy	• Mistrust and anxiety are sources of energy to the individual leader. If the URB scores are higher, role clarity and status become a source of energy; if the USD scores are higher, then agency, passion, power to regulate and vigilance become a source of energy for the individual.	• Trust, dialog and purpose become a source of energy to the individual leader. Transparency and space add to this energy.
Nature of relationships	Based on clarity of role expectations and clear differentiation in status and power	• Egalitarian and focused on mutual trust and respect
Basis of decision making	Either on the basis of personal judgment and discretion OR strictly by the book	• Dialog, participation and negotiation that enable shared ownership of the decision.

Table 7.6 Orientation of Indian managers in the third polarity

Dimension	SC	SI	OP
Control	49.08	47.00	54.98
Empowerment	49.07	52.10	51.38

Note: Each score is on a 0–100 scale.

- In such a scenario, the individual feels the need to have more control but is either reluctant or unable to exercise it.
- Not surprisingly, the EUM-O data suggest that our respondents would like their organizations to be more *Disciplined*. Simultaneously, our respondents feel the need to be more *Tough*. The overall picture seems to be of a person who feels the need for more control but is unable to empower him- or herself to exercise it.
- This difficulty for Indian managers is perhaps rooted in this low sense of empowerment. The EUM-O data suggest that most of our respondents find their organizations to be overly hierarchical and under-empowering. Our experience suggests that this feeling of a lack of empowerment does not stem only from inadequate structurally delegated authority but also has strong emotive undertones. We have often come across instances where people do not feel empowered even if structural authority is delegated to them. Thus, a selection committee may be delegated the authority to choose the right person, but its actual decision making may be based on factors other than its own judgment. Similarly, many managers feel it "safe" to sound their superior(s) before exercising even the legitimate authority that has been delegated to them.
- Thus, looking at the issue of empowerment only through the lens of structural delegation may not be very meaningful and, in fact, may be counterproductive. Delegation without empowerment diffuses accountability. While, theoretically, the person who has been delegated can be held accountable, the concerned person rarely has the complete psychological ownership. From the person's point of view, the decision is not really his or hers, though he or she may have signed on the dotted line. On the other hand, the person or persons who may actually be responsible have no formal role and, hence, cannot be held accountable.

Thus, issues of empowerment necessarily entail going beyond issues of structure and looking at the emotive/cultural dimension. Our hypothesis is that given the high relational orientation in the Indian psyche, the issue of empowerment is strongly impacted by two interrelated themes:

- The relationship matrix and its ambiance
- Psychological ownership of the system

For most Indian managers, the feeling of empowerment is intimately linked to the quality of their relationship with significant others particularly their boss. If they believe that they enjoy the goodwill and support of their boss, they feel empowered; otherwise, they do not. While relationship with the boss is the most significant element, it is by no means the only one. In fact, excessive closeness with the boss can alienate the individual from his or her peer group, causing a need to perpetually look behind one's back. Simply put, it is not just one relationship but an entire matrix in which the individual places him- or herself. It is the ambience of this container that determines the nature of empowerment that can flourish.

The other significant issue pertains to the psychological ownership of the system. Exercising power inevitably carries the risk of transgressing boundaries. Consequently, a feeling of legitimacy is integral to feeling empowered and exercising power. In the Indian context, this legitimacy is derived from "ownership of the system". There are two distinct aspects of it:

- Sense of belonging and commitment to the system (I belong to the system)
- Claim over the system and consequent presumption of right to act on its behalf (system belongs to me)

Given the higher UBP than USD orientation in the Indian psyche, the first part comes quite easily to most Indians. However, the situation in terms of the second aspect is complex. The claim/right over the system tends to be defined in absolute terms of "all or none". Either the person says that the system does not belong to me and I am only a "loyal servant" OR that I am the "master" and, hence, have complete ownership of the system. Thus, it is not surprising that many Indian organizations, irrespective of their formal structure, operate as a "collation of fiefdoms". In order to have "exclusive ownership", the chief of these fiefdoms tends to become the main boundary keeper who regulates all transactions between "inside" and "outside". A process that we saw in the way Ravi ran his factory in the Ravi–Hema case.

In such a scenario, the only person who can feel empowered is the "chief", whose sense of empowerment is also restricted to his or her own fiefdom, beyond which he or she feels as disempowered as others.

This drama is played out at all levels in the organization, and hence, the feeling of disempowerment prevails irrespective of the level of the person in the organizational hierarchy.

It is not uncommon for even very senior managers (including CEOs of large corporate houses) to express sentiments that one would associate with lower- or middle-level managers. Managers who do not feel empowered themselves can scarcely help others (including their subordinates) to feel empowered.

The end result is that in spite of all the right noises (and, in most cases, honest intentions) and all the systemic mechanisms, the ironical situation where feelings of inadequate control and inadequate empowerment continue to coexist.

4. Objective rationality versus Subjective sensing

All systems have a tangible and manifest reality that can be directly observed, measured, analyzed and placed under logical categories. Simultaneously, systems have a latent and intangible side that can only be sensed, intuitively grasped, and that defies logical/analytical categorization. The former calls for engagement with our "left brain", whereas the latter requires the deployment of our "right brain". It is now fairly well established that in any human interaction what is apparent and visible is only the "tip of the iceberg".

The actual dynamics is being directed not just by the logical arguments being traded but equally by the underlying feelings, beliefs, prejudices, preferences, motives and so on. No system can afford to ignore either the manifest or the latent. When the manifest is not engaged with it leads to arbitrariness, loss of pragmatism and irrationalities. On the other hand, when the latent is ignored, it leads to sterility, mediocrity and sudden eruptions and breakdowns. The manifest reality requires engagement with objective rationality, whereas the latent reality calls for deployment of subjective sensing, and leadership entails co-holding the two and managing their inevitable tension.

Leaders who lean towards the side of objective rationality prefer to work in a planned manner and strive towards goal-directed movement with clear action points. Their decision making is governed by objective, tangible and measurable factors. They tend to relate in a functional but depersonalized manner. While they are comfortable in exchange of ideas and thoughts, expressing and receiving of feelings does not come easily to them. They believe that human beings are primarily governed by rational self-interest, and hence, in their deliberations, they are guided by the issues at hand and pay scant attention to the underlying dynamics of feelings and relationships. They are likely to be most effective in situations that are amenable to a systematic and planned way of functioning, with clearly defined ground rules and degrees of freedom available to them. Too much rigidity is likely to suffocate them, and fuzzy situations are likely to leave them feeling confused.

A typical statement about Self and Others by a leader who leans towards objective rationality is likely to read as shown in Box 7.7.

Box 7.7   Objective rationality-centric

I rely on logic and reason in my dealings and decision making rather than emotional appeals. I am hardnosed about seeking and pursuing data and believe that numbers/data don't mislead, unlike personal opinions that may be tainted by feelings. In working with plans and programs, I invest energy in discussing or reviewing our measurement mechanisms. I lean more on the side of the tangible and material when I look for signs of progress. I don't have patience for those who cannot make a clear business case. I tend to trust action and outcomes more than intentions.

In the EUM framework, these leaders have a strong URB and UPA orientation.

Leaders who lean towards the side of subjective sensing tend to rely more on their intuition and hunches rather than on cold logic. They are comfortable with ambiguity and are generally willing to take unplanned exploratory steps. They pay great attention to their own feelings and are generally quick to pick up how other people are feeling and the dynamics of relationships. Their belief is that human beings are primarily governed by their feelings and conditioning received from their context.

Consequently, they place considerable emphasis on understanding the context rather than uniform and standardized application of rules and norms. Such leaders tend to be extremely effective in complex situations requiring nuanced understanding particularly of human dynamics, provided they have enough elbow room. Situations that are tightly defined in terms of rules and procedures tend to stifle them.

A typical statement about Self and Others by leaders who lean towards subjective sensing is likely to read as shown in Box 7.8.

Box 7.8   Subjective sensing-centric

I tend to view reality as more than just what is material and measurable. It includes the diverse views of people (and mine) from multiple standpoints, feelings and intuitions. I tend to be inclusive and open myself to others' experiences, perspectives and preferences. I don't seek out one best way or the right way and instead examine my choices and decisions against my evocations and my 'sense' of what *feels* right. In the face of incomplete information, I tell myself and others that it is important to trust oneself and make the judgment calls as required.

In the EUM framework, these leaders have a greater orientation towards USD, UMI and UDS and, at best, a moderate leaning towards URB. Table 7.7 illustrates the two dimensions.

The Indian Experience: what our data reveal

The scores of Indian managers on these two dimensions are summarized in Table 7.8.

Our data suggest that Indian managers have a marked preference for objective rationality. The SC scores for objective rationality are much higher than for subjective sensing. The gap further widens in SI.

These managers also see it as a significant differentiator between themselves and others. Of all the eight dimensions, the gap between SC and OP is highest in case of objective rationality (14.13).

• To what extent this identification and valuing translates into actual behavior is somewhat debatable. In our experience of working with Indian managers, we have found them swearing

Table 7.7 Objective rationality versus subjective sensing

Dimension	Objective rationality	Subjective sensing
Tilt towards Universes	• Strong affinity towards URB and UPA and not more than moderate leaning towards USD	Strong affinity towards USD, UMI and UDS and not more than moderate leaning towards URB
Purpose	To focus on the tangible/measurable goals and clearly defined milestones	• To focus on the essence/spirit and their subjective interpretation of the task
Source of energy	Situations which are amenable to goal-directed movement with clarity of the end state and the way forward	• Complex, hazy situations which require exploration and experimentation.
Nature of relationships	Functional, transactional and depersonalized with clear expectations	• Intimate, personalized with fuzzy boundaries
Basis of decision making	Empirical data and explicitly stated criteria like benchmarks, market research, survey data, etc.	• Intuitive sense making, leaps of faith and personal preferences

Table 7.8 Orientation of Indian managers in the fourth polarity

Dimension	SC	SI	OP
Objective rationality	65.37	63.34	51.24
Subjective sensing	37.74	30.52	39.30

Note: Each score is on a 0–100 scale.

strongly by objective rationality, but *their actual behavior is often determined by subjective sensing.*

• This is difficult to acknowledge because for many of them, *subjectivity* is a bad word associated primarily with bias and prejudice. In their effort to demonstrate that they are free of any prejudice, they often take considerable trouble to claim that their stances are being governed only by cold logic. We have often found that it is virtually impossible to convince many Indian managers through rational argument. Given their intellectual acumen, they are able to "manufacture" logic, to defend virtually any position no matter how untenable it may seem to others. On the other hand, it is much easier to influence them through striking an emotional chord. Establishing a personalized connect often becomes a precondition to soliciting any help/cooperation. The same person who may stubbornly refute all rational arguments can suddenly change his or her stance with a plea like "Please find a way to help me out".

- There is perhaps an implicit recognition of this process as evidenced by the relatively lower score in OP for objective rationality. Clearly, it is easier to see the absence of "objective rationality" in others than in oneself.

- The process of "rationalization" is not unique to India, nor is the fact that feelings, needs and values play a much bigger role in the influence process as compared to logical reasoning. These phenomena can be witnessed in every part of the world, but what makes them more pronounced in India (particularly in the corporate world) is the immense difficulty in acknowledging the role of one's own subjective feelings and holding them as undesirable. Thus, the word *Emotional* figures much lower in SC than does *Rational* and goes down even more in SI.

We suspect that this disdain towards subjective sensing may be a protective device to ensure that our innate pull towards subjective sensing (arising out of features such as context sensitivity, primacy of belonging, faith, androgyny, etc.) can be kept under check and do not interfere with the what we believe is a necessary feature of the corporate world viz. allegiance to objective rationality.

Overall picture

Table 7.9 summarizes the orientation of the Indian managers with respect to the eight dimensions covered by us.

The broad picture is of a person who regards his or her objective rationality as the main source of pride. Not merely are the others seen as less objective and rational but also as people who are not very high on subjective sensing either. The OP scores on

Table 7.9 Leadership orientation of the Indian manager

Orientation	Identification	Compared to Others	Feelings that it generates
Preservation	Moderate identification	MORE than others	Seen as a liability
Transformation	Moderate identification	LESS than others	Aspired for
Meritocracy	Moderate identification on the higher side but...	LESS than others	Aspired for
Humanistic	Low identification but...	MORE than others	Seen as a liability
Control	Moderate identification	LESS than others	Seen as a necessary evil
Empowerment	Moderate identification	LESS than others	Aspired for
Objective rationality	High identification	MORE than others	Area of pride
Subjective sensing	Low identification	LESS than other	Seen as undesirable

subjective sensing are higher than SC but quite low in absolute terms (39.3). Consequently, the person is likely to operate from the stance of "I know better". While the person wishes to translate this "superior understanding" into action effectiveness, there are some difficulties being experienced in this endeavor. This is evidenced by the fact that in all three aspirational dimensions (transformation, meritocracy and empowerment) SC scores are lower than OP scores.

The person also believes that preservation-centricity and humanistic orientation are his or her nemeses that must be overcome. There is a wish to feel more empowered but reluctance to exercise subjective sensing/personal power and, hence, perhaps an inadequate sense of being "on top of one's situation".

Revisiting the uneasy relationship

The picture painted earlier is perhaps a by-product of the uneasy relationship between Hema and Ravi who reside within the Indian manager to varying degrees. Hema with her leaning towards transformation and meritocracy feels contemptuous towards Ravi's "frog-in-the-well" orientation. She may look at him as a relic of the past, but she can't escape the reality that he is very much there, that he enjoys high credibility in the system and that he has the credentials to back it up.

For Ravi, Hema is an unwelcome intruder who has been thrust on him. He may see her as an upstart who has no idea of the "ground realities", but there is no way he can escape her dynamism, her wider perspective, her self-confidence and the power advantage she enjoys over him.

Often, both Hema and Ravi get caught in the stance of "I know better" and focus on "solving the problem" that is posed by the other. Hema tries to get rid of Ravi or sideline him or try to get him out of his comfort zone through developmental inputs like management programs, coaching and so on.

Ravi, on his part, sometimes plays along, toes the line, or withdraws and sulks in a corner or tries to undermine Hema in a subtle manner. Irrespective of how the tension of this relationship is coped by the individual concerned, the creative potential inherent in this tension is rarely harnessed.

We believe that this unease has tremendous creative potential. Harnessing this potential entails moving beyond the realm of attitudes and behavior and understanding/engaging with the "perspectives" that Hema and Ravi hold. The differences in their perspectives stem from the differences between the civilizational identity akin to India of ages and corporate social character, which is largely driven by Anglo-Saxon management thoughts and is reinforced by globalization and liberal consumerism.

In an earlier chapter, we had offered our understanding of how the Indian managers are impacted by their cultural context. However, human beings are impacted not just by their personal and cultural context but also by the imperatives of the times that they live in and the social/structural arrangement of which they are a part.

Eric Fromm[1] has used the term *social character*, which is shaped by this social arrangement. He describes it as "the essential nucleus of the character structure of most members of the group which has developed as the result of the basic experiences and mode of life common to that group".

Every social arrangement is based on and sustained by values and beliefs that are consistent with it. For example, a feudal structure requires that people believe in "the divine right to rule". An autocratic regime is easy to maintain if people regard obedience as a highly valued virtue and have a belief in the benevolence of the autocrat. For people who are outside the social arrangement, these values and beliefs may seem odd, but for those who are part of the social design, its underlying values and beliefs seem as "self-evident truths".

Thus, for most of us who live in a democratic, capitalistic society, its underlying values and beliefs, such as equality, liberty and autonomy, among others, seem unquestionable, which for people who lived at a different point in human history would seem very odd. Many of them may be "shocked" to know that people belonging to different classes, gender, races, castes and so on can be regarded as "equal".

The corporate world is also a social arrangement with its own set of values and beliefs and, hence, fosters a "social character" that is best suited for its sustenance. Thus, while individual organizations differ from each other in terms of their history, ethos, culture, practices and the like, these differences are held within a broad container that may be called "the corporate way". Thus, it is rather unlikely that there would be many organizations that would not put emphasis on features such as meritocracy, continuous improvement and the like.

On the assumption that the "idealized self" of most of our respondents would be heavily influenced by what they believe will work in their context, it would be reasonable to take the collective SI scores as a reflection of the corporate social character.

Going by this reasoning as also our collective experience, we believe that the prevalent position of corporate social character in terms of the four basic polarities is as follows:

- There is a distinct tilt towards transformation as compared to preservation. Tradition is held with ambivalence or shame or self-hate – transformation is seen as a redemption from it.
- Meritocracy is valued more than humanistic values. Life is seen primarily through the utilitarian lens, and humanistic values are regarded as 'means' for becoming more effective.
- There is a distinct preference for objective rationality over subjective sensing. The notion of truth and basis for action are seen through determinism – a by-product of classical Newtonian physics – and intuitive subjectivity is held with mistrust and cynicism.

- Empowerment is seen as a necessity for managing and exercising control in a large complex context with multiple stakeholders. The basic purpose is to ensure that things happen in accordance with a preset plan/intent.

Needless to say, the preceding points are not applicable to every corporate executive but should be taken as a broad pattern. Also, these preferences may not be confined only to the corporate world and may be reflective of the times that we live in. However, there can be little doubt in terms of their applicability to the corporate world.

If these polarities are mapped against the features of Indian identity described in Chapter 6, a very different picture would emerge. Given features like relational orientation, context-specificity, androgyny, emphasis on selflessness and renunciation, discomfort with dynamic masculinity and so on, the Indian psyche would feel more at home in a setting where the emphasis is on preservation, humanistic values, subjective sensing and readiness to go with the flow.

Thus, the "self-evident truths" by which Ravi lives are quite different from those of Hema. Often, these two sets of truths reside within the same individual – one set of truths stem from the civilization identity and another from the corporate social character. The civilizational quintessence pulls the individual in one direction, and the contextual imperatives of the corporate world, in another. Furthermore, most of them also seem to believe that their civilizational quintessence is a liability, which they can neither embrace nor fully discard. This makes the task of balancing/co-holding the two perspectives even more difficult.

Balancing and/or co-holding

Polarities are inevitable – we have no choice but to manage them through co-holding and/or striking a balance between them. Balancing and co-holding are not mutually exclusive, but there is an important difference between them.

- In balancing, the two poles are locked in a distributive (zero-sum) relationship, whereas in co-holding they are held in an integrative (non-zero-sum) relationship. Balancing requires the manager or leader to compensate for an earlier tilt towards one of the polarities with effort and energy towards the other.

Co-holding entails trying to engage with them in a manner that they become supportive rather than antagonistic of each other. For example, if a manager seeks to balance empowerment and control, he or she would structure tasks and efforts in a way that some are controlled and some of these are offered as sops for excessive control or empowered. On the other hand, a manager who wishes to co-hold will try to control in a manner (e.g., through guidance, directions, boundary setting, review, etc.) that enhances empowerment rather than curtailing it.

- Thus, in balancing, paying attention to one entails neglect of the other, whereas in co-holding, one can work towards simultaneous enhancement of both. This difference becomes clear, if we see how the control–empowerment polarity seems to be currently engaged with by Indian managers. As argued earlier, in the present scenario both sides are neglected; there is neither adequate control nor adequate Empowerment.
- In the EUM framework, balancing is associated with URB and co-holding with UDS. As our data suggest that at present, the Indian managers are more focused on balancing than on co-holding.

Balancing is, of course, critical to management of polarities, but it is not enough. While balancing helps in coping with the situation, it is through co-holding that the creative potential can be unlocked. However, so long as we engage with a polarity only at the level of attitude and behavior, we will not be able to go beyond balance/compromise. Co-holding will require an engagement at the level of the underlying perspective, that is, the self-evident truths on which the polarity stands. The movement towards co-holding will entail engagement with what we have called the tension arising out of different perspectives underlying civilizational quintessence and imperatives of the corporate world. In order to do this, we need a deeper and empathetic exploration of the nature of the difference between the two perspectives. In the next chapter, we have tried to look at the three important strands of these two perspectives.

Note

1 Fromm, E. (1941). *Escape from Freedom*. New York: Ferrar & Rinehart.

Chapter 8

Two perspectives

In several places in this book we have referred to two hypothetical characters – Ravi and Hema.

We have suggested that they are not two different types of people but symbols of two forces that operate within the modern-day Indian managers: Ravi represents the pull of their civilizational codings, and Hema represents the imperatives of the modern-day corporate world that are largely derived from management paradigms based on Anglo-Saxon thinking. The rise of this genre of management thinking, spanning across universities and business schools on both sides of the Atlantic, has been impressive in the way it has pervaded and impacted our ways of engaging with the world of business organizations.

There is a shared management paradigm that has gotten created and integrated by businesses worldwide over the past two centuries. It is not surprising that entrepreneurs and management professionals across small and large businesses worldwide share similar perspectives and perhaps identical lens towards growth, strategy and wealth creation in a globalized world. This paradigm has led to the emergence of a shared language that links business professionals worldwide.

In this chapter, we would like to argue that this management paradigm rests on a perspective (which we will refer to as P1) that is quite different from the perspective that people like Ravi hold (which we will refer to as P2). These two perspectives are based on different sets of assumptions about human existence, nature of technology and nature of human collectives. In the following paragraphs, we explore three main strands of the difference between the two perspectives.

Strand I

The homo economicus versus the homo reciprocans

As early as in 1836, J. S. Mill,[1] in his writing on political economy, proposed a new definition of "*Man*" – who is self-centered, rational and averse to labor or at least wishing to minimize it, as the subject of political economics. Many of the traditional economists, including Ricardo and Adam Smith, endorsed this concept. The birth and growth of Homo economicus were aided by the Industrial Revolution, during which traditional feudal agrarian economies were being dismantled and replaced by the new ways of thinking and creating value.

Over the years, market capitalism has endorsed, evoked and promoted this notion of and associated values, biases and symbolism of the Homo economicus – a term used for this new model of Homo sapiens – "*that acts to obtain the highest possible well-being for himself or herself, given available information about opportunities and other constraints, both natural and institutional, on his or her ability to achieve predetermined goals*".

Founded on the work of Aristotle and later by political economist John Stuart Mill, and then subsequently glamorized by Ayn Rand in her works, including *Atlas Shrugged* and *The Virtue of Selfishness*, the Homo economicus is seen as 'rational' and 'self-centered' and as playing two key roles in modern society:

* That of a discerning consumer where he or she maximizes utility
* That of an ambitious producer, where he or she maximizes profits

Till the 1980s, the Homo economicus was yet to make a grand entry into the Indian context, though the fledgling private sector and the nascent management institutes were joining hands in heralding and celebrating it. However, liberalization in the early 1990s ushered in and accentuated a legitimate shift towards looking at oneself through the lens of Homo economicus. Many of the educated, competent, meritocratic and the middle classed were getting recruited and socialized by global firms that were steeped in this philosophy.

It was not just organizations that reinforce this lens of Homo economicus, but schools, colleges and even the so-called nuclear families are also pushing the young Indian into being self-serving and utility maximizing. By the turn of the century, the acronym 'WIIFM' or 'what's in it for me?', was getting accepted and steadily integrated into the language of all – the young and the old, the urban and the rural, men or women.

This accentuation of the Homo economicus over the last two decades, we believe, is generating intense inner conflict, tremendous anxiety and turmoil in many a Ravi, for this contradicts if not demolishes their notions of role taking, values systems, and nature of communities.

The Homo Economicus is steadily displacing the traditional Homo Reciprocans, and rendering it as irrelevant and insignificant in these times!

Who is the Homo reciprocans?

Reciprocity in the traditional sense refers to a non–market exchange economy where profit is not as critical as a fair redistribution of finished goods in a community. In reciprocal societies and communities, exchange is impacted and governed by social relationships – and social relationships are based on *kinship*. Reciprocity gave rise to the traditional Homo reciprocans.

The Homo reciprocans acts out in the following ways:

- First, the Homo reciprocans invests into dyadic social relationships where one gives gifts to friends and potential enemies in order to establish a relationship by placing them in debt.
- When the exchange is delayed or incomplete, it creates both a social relationship as well as an obligation for a return (i.e., debt). It enables the person to establish hierarchy if the debt is not repaid. The failure to make a return may end a relationship between equals.
- These social relationships and the consequent complexities are unequivocally managed by the Homo reciprocans. The traditional Indian manager deployed these to manage complex hierarchies as well as dysfunctional processes and feelings of rivalry, envy, insecurities, anxieties, competitiveness and so on.

An easy example of such dyadic relationships is around the process of performance management involving a supervisor and a subordinate. Often the supervisor would invest into this relationship by offering a gift – a generous appraisal in which the exchange is incomplete or at best delayed. The subordinate then carries a debt or an obligation that renders a power dynamic that can be easily contrasted to a Western definition of *professionalism*.

To someone like Hema, this process would appear as 'nepotistic' or even corrupt – but to Ravi – it is but a means of managing complex systems.

- Another form of reciprocity that the Homo reciprocans invests into is the traditional system of 'pooling'. Traditionally the Indian understands and internalizes the impact of deprivation and paucity, and the coping mechanisms of pooling which are governed by the Dharma of holding and balancing Self and systemic needs. Pooling allows for understanding the fine tension between individual and collective desires and needs.

The traditional *Jajmani* system[2] is an important example of pooling as it performed important functions and roles that were both economic and social. The pooling of resources served to maintain the Indian village as a self-sufficient unit built on caste and community interdependency.

In the recent years, joint families, for example, in most parts of the country deploy subjective wisdom in sustaining and institutionalizing reciprocity within the system. The Homo reciprocans comes in with this ancient and traditional context of pooling.

An easy illustration of 'pooling' is how the traditional brick and mortar organizations would look at the prospect of budgeting and allocations. What would be deemed as critical would be the notion of equalization in terms of access to resources, as opposed to only a meritocratic view of what deserves better resources. Resource allocation in the traditional system as opposed to the modern management perspectives would be imbued by relationships, debt and obligation and a sense of pooling.

Again, modern management theories constructed on Homo economicus would look at pooling as a source of waste and inefficiencies.

The main differences between the Homo economicus and Homo reciprocans and consequent impact on management are summarized in Table 8.1.

Most anthropologists believe that industrial and postindustrial societies have experienced a cleavage from traditional societies and from the notion of reciprocity.

Table 8.1 Comparing the Homo economicus with the Homo reciprocans

The Homo economicus	The Homo reciprocans
Rationality and self-centredness form the foundation for management thinking	Kinship and communities form the boundary for management thinking
Agency and individual power/ desire is celebrated	Sacrifice towards the larger good or the community is celebrated
Hierarchy gets created through expertise and knowledge	Hierarchy gets created through obligation and unequal gifting
Contracted deliverables and negotiated deals determine roles, relatedness and relationships	Gifting determines roles, relatedness and relationships
Performance is seen and valued as a tangible process	Performance and associated management of it is seen as a social process
Motivation is individualized and on the basis of individual desire	Motivation is built through commitment to collective and kinship interests

This has resulted in atomization of human behavior, especially when economics is separated from culture and promoting 'under-socialization'. This is where the previously mentioned cleavage creates a culture of 'individualism' sans a human connect – of island-hood and alienation.

Our experience with the EUM framework shows that the kinship and its consequent notions of reciprocity have not disappeared but only lie dormant, and hence, most Indian managers try to co-hold them along with the need to forge relationships around competency, knowledge, skills and diversity propounded by needs of meritocracy. We have encountered many effective managers who are able to co-hold/balance these divergent pulls, and this ability plays a significant role in their effectiveness as managers and leaders. However, there are also many other managers who remain caught in ambivalence and find it difficult to embrace both the

Homo economicus (because of cultural codings) and the Homo reciprocans (because of the prevalent management paradigms). The end result is that both tendencies operate in an insidious manner, creating dysfunctional processes.

Some of these are detailed in the following subsections.

I. Shadow of the Homo economicus

Given our uneasy relationship with USD, many Indian managers carry some discomfort with the Homo economicus perspective, both for themselves and in their relatedness with others. Consequently, WIIFM is not direct and up front but subtle and insidious. The individual needs a systemic justification for the pursuit of self-interest. Thus, the "rational" pursuit of self-interest becomes the "rationalized" pursuit of self-interest. Self-interest is pursued but in the garb of systemic needs and collective good.

Simultaneously we find a conscious distancing from a key archetypal identity form, namely, that of the self-sacrificing hero. In India, this archetypal identity was not merely revered through mythological characters like Rama, Bharat and Sravan Kumar, among others, but also celebrated through fictional characters in films and literature. The renowned actor late Balraj Sahni had come to be so identified with this identity that in various films (*Bhabi, Chhoti Behen, Seema, Do Raaste*, to name a few) he was repeatedly depicted as a highly altruistic and compassionate character, who would be regarded as almost an antithesis of Homo economicus. Often this identity was juxtaposed against a Homo economicus character who was invariably depicted as selfish and divisive.

It is therefore quite revealing that in the EUM data, *Sacrificing* appears a distant last in both SI and OP. Even in SC, it is only slightly higher and remains second to last. Our hypothesis is that this distancing from the archetype of self-sacrificing protagonist serves two purposes:

1   It reminds the individual that he or she is in a Homo economicus context and therefore must be watchful of the civilizational codings that may propel him or her towards Homo reciprocans.
2   It allows him or her to exploit this archetypal identity in other people – after all, it is the individual's responsibility to look after self-interest, and if a person is not doing, so then it is perfectly legitimate to exploit him or her.

Today, this archetypal identity, which was once held in pride and dignity, is now held with disdain from a Homo economicus point of view. It is another matter that there are many organizations that consciously or unconsciously extract from this identity and create wealth under the banner of Homo economicus.

2. The shadow of Homo reciprocans

Traditionally, many Indian organizations, particularly the family managed ones, operated with kinship culture – offering a sense of belonging, loyalty and emotional infrastructure. While these had their own share of dysfunctionalities, sadly, with the advent of "professionalism", these benefits are seen as inconsequential today.

However, the need for them has not disappeared and they can often be seen at work even in the so-called modern companies. It is therefore not surprising that our experience, as well as the EUM data from the new-age companies, is not significantly different from the traditional companies.

What is interesting to note is that the set of new-age companies, the global organizations and the unicorns, while explicitly stating their pro-diversity philosophy and their bias for the Homo economicus, actually end up grappling with processes of kinship and gifting as well. These processes are held as *taboo* under the new lens and yet survive below the radar or the modern lens of fairness and openness.

Some such examples include the following:

- Reciprocity and kinship would be invested in by a manager in the form of gifting opportunities for 'on-site assignments' or 'high-technology projects' to colleagues from the same socioeconomic-cultural background.
- Reciprocity would be reinforced through the formation of cliques and clans within the organizations that go beyond modern resourcing algorithms. For example, often the member of the clan would not be released on account of kinship.
- Often the Homo reciprocans would use reciprocity and gifting for building expertise and knowledge across teams – quite different from how Homo economicuses would anchor the same processes.

While ostensibly, the modern Indian organization would argue for innovation, diversity and knowledge – the 'shadow' of gifting and building kinship through reciprocity is always flowing below the surface. Worse still, this shadow is feared or seen as 'impure' and, while constantly repressed, seems to haunt many an Indian manager.

3. Negative reciprocity

Negative reciprocity is the attempt to get "something for nothing with impunity". It may be described as 'haggling', 'barter', or 'theft'. It is the most impersonal and extractive form of exchange, with interested parties seeking to maximize their gains.

Since negative reciprocity comes closest to the notion of Homo economicus, it often serves as the lowest common denominator, and thus, the individual does not feel divided within. He or she draws solace from the philosophical strands of modern capitalism, where greed and negative reciprocity are held as desirable values and preconditions for success. While this rationalization silences the Homo reciprocans within, it leaves the residues of guilt and loneliness for the individual to grapple with, for it reduces everything – "including human beings" – to mere commodities. Terms such as *talent management* and *resource management* that are applied to human beings are a stark example of this phenomenon.

To sum up, Indian managers seem uncomfortable both with the Homo economicus and reciprocans. This ambivalence creates all kinds of difficulties for them but is also a blessing in disguise. It propels them to find ways and means of co-holding the two. In our experience, it is managers and leaders who manage to do it effectively are most likely to succeed in the Indian context.

Strand 2

The Rational Ingenieur versus the Bricoleur

Hema and Ravi also differ in their mental models around task and technology. Ravi is a product of a certain quintessential Indian way of working whereas Hema subscribes to a body of knowledge, which is the foundation of current management practice world over.

Over the years, a body of knowledge around management tools, frameworks and approaches, including Management By Objectives (MBO), Business Process Reengineering (BPR), Strategic Thinking,

Waterfall Model for IT projects, Core Competencies, Six Sigma and Financial Leverage, among others, have emerged worldwide. This body of knowledge has enabled businesses worldwide to create wealth. It has led to the design of curriculums in business schools. It has influenced how leadership has been defined in the current context.

In terms of the content, these diverse tools and approaches may seem quite unrelated to each other, but there exists many a common thread that point to a paradigm or a mental model that has enabled and enlivened the body.

One of the common threads that connects these tools and their deployment in the present-day world is the notion or archetype of '*Rational Ingenieur*' or the 'Rational Engineer'. By Rational Ingenieur, we refer to the one who uses or drives the *engine*. The Industrial Revolution has seeded this paradigm, which has driven globalization and designed the engines of its growth and scalability in the business world. Within this paradigm, logic, rationality, blueprints, standard operating procedures (SOPs) and goal-driven purposive behavior are celebrated.

Positioned as a gift of Western scientific knowledge, the Rational Ingenieur has been energetically subscribed to by ruling elite and middle class in India, especially given the fact we had missed out on the magic of Industrial Revolution because of our colonized past. It has become an inner archetype as well as an aspired role model that can energize Indian society towards development, prosperity and growth and that can transcend us from the limitations of past knowledge that could not discern scientific rigor from mere common sense. By embellishing objectivity, data, goals, algorithms, linear cause–effect models, and long-range thinking, the Rational Ingenieur reinforces a sense of confidence to become masters of our own destiny.

However, along with the excitement of subscribing to this new faith, for many Indians, like Ravi, it has also created inner turmoil and unease. It creates confusion on how we value our legacy – an inheritance that did not exactly complement the new knowledge systems often leading to feelings of inferiority and inadequacy. It also creates a split between our internal preferences and espoused methods. People like Ravi don't think in terms of scenarios and grandiose plans. They like to focus on "what is", "what is available" and "what best can be done with it". Their preference is for "doing the best that they can" and accepting reality as it emerges.

Their mental models are best captured by what Levi Strauss has described as the Bricoleur.

Introducing the alternative paradigm: the Bricoleur

Levi Strauss[3] spoke of an alternate mind-set in his famed work – *The Savage Mind* – formulating and introducing the term *Bricolage* as he argues on behalf of the traditional and non- Western knowledge systems that have existed over centuries. Having researched on American Indian body of knowledge, Levi Strauss formulated Bricolage as "*the process of **evolution** not as a product of design or an unfolding of a predetermined plan or template – but rather as the makeshift adaptation of existing structures and functions to new ends*".

It was his definition of *Bricoleur* that caught our attention, and Table 8.2 summarizes our understanding of the two terms *Bricoleur* and *Bricolage* to the Rational Ingenieur.

Indianness and Bricolage

As we look at bricolage and the bricoleur in the context of civilizational predispositions of Indian managers, there are several themes that stand out.

a   The first theme pertains to the significance of 'surrender' to the process of evolution, value creation or bricolage. In contrast, the Rational Ingenieur's mind-set is focused on the notion of control.

The modern organization for example not only echoes the machine mind-set but, more important, it also runs from a *control* principle – and that this control is reinforced through 'rationality' and 'engineering', giving rise to the powerful mind-set of the Rational Ingenieur. As the EUM data shows, many of our respondents experience some angst and anxiety arising out of the "need to control" and their experience of "not being able to control". Often these fears and anxieties stymie any real spontaneity and aliveness within the system.

b   The second theme that differentiates the Rational Ingenieur in a very Indian context is the unease the with **finiteness** of resources – modernity almost lends itself a belief of infinite

Table 8.2 Comparing the Rational Ingenieur with the Bricoleur

The Rational Ingenieur	The Bricoleur
Is someone who works as a thinking person, drawing on the method or the process of throughputs; displays rigor and discipline	Is someone who works with his or her hands and is willing to engage in roundabout ways of working; displays a sense of opportunism and a sense of deviousness at times
Is someone who desires and needs an infrastructure and resources critical to the throughput	Is comfortable using 'odds and ends', for there is nothing literally at hand. Is comfortable and committed to 'what is available' as well as with the experience of deprivation
Leverages and deploys 'rational thinking' and, in this course, becomes rigid and bounded; does not trust feelings and intuition	Is someone who thinks, feels and acts 'flexibly' – is not a slave to rigidity
Prefers complexity	Likes to keep things 'simple'
Is constrained by rules, methods and paradigms; does not trust any knowledge that is not explicit	Follows his or her own heart and deploys subjective wisdom
Invests in gaining 'control' over the resources and the means of production or throughput	Becomes an 'agent' of Bricolage (evolution), and is willing to 'surrender'; believes that the Bricolage operates through him or her

resources, while the Bricoleur seems a lot more at ease with and accepting of *deprivation*.

We believe this to be a crucial strand of Indianness. The Bricoleur identity does not see deprivation or finiteness of resources as a curse but more of an acceptance of 'what is'. Thus, transformation is not seen merely as a masculine form of transcendence but a feminine acceptance of immanence.

c   Last, an acceptance of **self-doubt** – an inner ambivalence towards the notions of Truth and reality contrasts the Bricoleur from the Rational Ingenieur. For the Rational Ingenieur, Truth is absolute, and hence, one must arrive at certainty and be clear about what one is doing. The Bricoleur does not carry any compulsion to polarize the ambivalence and is ready to deal with the uncertainty, which is inherent in evolution. The Rational Ingenieur needs a "blueprint" whereas the Bricoleur is happy to explore and engage with the emergent reality. Given the leaning towards context sensitivity, this lack of absoluteness comes a lot more easily to us, yet the context-free ways of the Rational Ingenieur require us to push aside the "self-doubt" and pretend to be more clear and definite than how we actually feel.

Thus, our hypothesis is that Indianness has a strong link to the Bricoleur mind-set and is yet grappling with modernity and its bias towards the Rational Ingenieur. In our work with Indian managers, and through the EUM framework, we witness a tension of subscribing to the Rational Ingenieur and co-holding the Bricoleur within.

Most modern managers and technocrats have demonstrated a strong bias towards the engineering mind-set and denied or repressed the Bricoleur within. However, they experience the consequences of this bias – including the anxiety around control, fear of obsolescence, fear of failure and a lack of faith in subjectivity and feelings. It is therefore not surprising that URB and UPA emerge as the two most identified with and valued Universes for our respondents. Also, both *Emotional* and *Uninhibited* (necessary prerequisites for spontaneity and subjective expression) are shunned by them.

Simultaneously, the Bricoleur seems to be making his or her presence felt in a significant way, though mostly outside the realm of large corporations. There have been many narratives – about ordinary, simple and relatively uneducated people; about 'commoners'; or about bourgeois who are not socialized to the paradigm of Rational Ingenieur or do not subscribe to its practice and method and yet have emerged with profoundly innovative and creative solutions.

Many of these innovations and solutions were built from existing resources and existing technologies and yet transformed not just the product but also the social relations. These outbursts of innovative solutions have been mapped, researched and dialogued on – these have been branded as **'Jugaad'** or the Indian school of innovation and have caught the attention of global academics.

In 2010, Harvard Business School added the case study *The Dabbawala System: On-Time Delivery, Every Time*[4] (2010) to its compendium for system's high level of service with a low-cost and simple operating system. The case study spoke about the efficiency and complexity of a process by which some 175,000 tiffin boxes were sorted, transported, delivered and returned each day by *people who were mostly illiterate and unsophisticated*.

The average literacy of the Dabbawalas was of passing eighth grade, and yet, here were a set of people who could boast of a Six Sigma process compliance of a complex supply chain model.

Jugaad or Indian Bricolage is increasingly accepted as a management technique and is recognized all over the world as an acceptable form of frugal engineering at its peak in India. Companies in India are adopting Jugaad as a practice to reduce R&D costs.

Our focus here is not on Jugaad but on the mental model, which underlies it and how this mental model can be valued and graced in organizations, which are largely built around the perspective of the Rational Ingenieur. What is important is to recognize that Bricolage entails a fundamentally different perspective to engagement with task, technology and resources. It entails a willingness to surrender, an acceptance of finiteness of resources, an acknowledgment of uncertainty and a willingness to go with the flow. It therefore threatens to create a psychic split between valuing traditional knowledge and the engineering mind-set as seen in the Hema–Ravi case.

This split is sometimes dealt with through jettisoning the Indianness within or at least marginalizing its impact in the task systems. The consequence of this process is that the privileged class of moneyed and educated technocrats and designers can collude with a school of looking at organizations and systems, which is largely based on the Rational Ingenieur perspective. Besides undermining the individual and systemic potential, this stance also contributes to holding Indianness with inferiority and shame.

Another implication is that the Bricoleur gets confined to small, informal spaces and his/her brand of innovation does not go beyond expedient solutions. Without the help and support of the Rational Ingenieur, there is no way the Bricoleur can actualize his or her potential.

We also believe that co-holding of the two is important not merely for developing and designing world-class organizations but also from the larger human perspective, considering that the consequences of the myth of infinite resources have already reached an alarming level.

Strand 3

The agonic versus the hedonic paradigm

A large part of management theory and practice uses the frameworks and language of warfare. It is not unusual to hear managers describe their competitors as "the enemy". While the need for collaboration is recognized, it is primarily directed inward. The relationship with the outside (particularly competition) is assumed to be hostile. Thus, "collaborate internally in order to compete externally" is likely to be regarded as a self-evident truth by most managers. The relationship with other stakeholders like customers, suppliers, external agencies is not seen as directly hostile, but given the basic Homo economicus assumption, there is an adversarial undercurrent to them. It would be a rare organization that would not try to get the upper hand or better part of the bargain in such relationships.

Ethologist Michael Chance[5] has classified two ways of looking at a collective – centripetal and acentric. A centripetal collective is organized with clearly defined roles and usually around one or more alpha male leaders. In contrast, an acentric collective is like a network – individualistic and loosely structured often bordering on anarchy.

Traditionally, most modern corporations would fall in the centripetal collective category, though increasingly we find a shift towards the acentric networks. Furthermore, Chance postulates two basic modes on which a centripetal arrangement is based and enlivened – agonic and hedonic.

The agonic mode is based upon the collective's perception and experience of threat, power and anxiety, whereas the hedonic mode is based on playful catching-up and prestige.

In the agonic mode, the group is essentially seen as a source of common defense. Consequently, the group is organized around that individual who has the greatest fighting capability and maximum resource holding potential (RHP). The intragroup relations are marked by mutual defensiveness and the group has to develop ways and means to ensure that the hostilities within the group are controlled and contained. This is achieved through a rigid pecking order, compliance and threat of punishment. The bonding between members is in the nature of an alliance against a potential enemy. All relationships are determined by the relative positions in respect of dominance and submission. Needless to say, that "aggression" and "RHP" are highly valued virtues in an agonic group. The more aggressive a member is and the greater is his or her RHP, the higher would be his or her self-esteem, status and entitlements to privileges.

In contrast, in the Hedonic mode, the group is a source of mutual confidence and the intragroup relations are marked by mutual dependence rather than mutual defensiveness. Consequently, such collectives are organized around the individual who has the maximum prestige rather than the one who is most aggressive or has maximum RHP. Prestige is derived either through altruistic acts or through demonstration of superior skills. The individual's effort is to maximize positive attention (e.g., being perceived as helpful and competent) rather than defensive attention (e.g., being perceived as potentially injurious).

Consequently, social behavior in hedonic mode is governed by signals of mutual assurance and support. Physical proximity, stroking, grooming, hugging and sharing are encouraged, and defensive behavior is deactivated. The emphasis is on exploration of the social environment without a major preoccupation with threats from within the group.

The difference between the two modes has been illustrated by Elaine Morgan[6] by contrasting baboons with gorillas and chimpanzees – "The baboon aspiring to dominance commands attention by biting and threat displays with his huge canine teeth". Consequently, among baboons,

[t]he males have to be bullies. The troop has to rally to them. And since not even baboons are born disciplined, discipline has to be inculcated. Females, juveniles and subordinates have to be taught their place, and frequently reminded of their place, by threats and punishments and bites on the neck. Usually they learn fast, and a display of fangs or the flash of an alpha's eyelids is enough to keep in line. As long as they remain in line, the alpha's rule is benevolent and administered through rough justice and old fashioned chivalry.

Morgan goes on to elaborate that the alpha baboon

will hog all the best food and impose his will brutally on weaker males. He demands instant and unquestioning obedience, and when danger threatens he will marshal his troops and stand up and fight like a hero, shoulder to shoulder with his loyal comrades.

Even under normal circumstances "deployment of a baboon troop on the move is governed by a complex system of rules dictating where everyone is in relation to the central hierarchy according to age, sex, status, competence and other variables".

In contrast, the gorillas and chimpanzees adopt a very different strategy to draw attention, gain prominence and achieve social stature. They do it through display, or showing off. Morgan describes this process as follows:

> They seek for ways of making themselves conspicuous: they bounce around and shake the branches. They find interesting objects, and their companions cluster around to see what they have got and what they are going to do with it. The dominant gorilla, the alpha silver back, of whom much is expected, has been seen to mount the most stupendous show stopping performances in this line.

Not surprisingly, the gorilla is often described as an inoffensive mild creature who lives in amiable serenity. Irven Devore[7] has this to say about the dominant male gorilla:

> His dominance over the group is absolute but normally genial . . .
> The leaders are usually quite approachable. Females nestle against them and infants crawl happily over their huge bodies. Amity reigns. When a band of gorillas is at rest, the young play, the mothers tend their infants, and the other adults lie at peace and soak up the sun.

A significant question is, Which of these two modes is more applicable to the *Homo sapiens*?

According to Morgan, while gorillas/chimpanzees are much closer to us in terms of evolutionary history, it is the baboon who has received the maximum attention by scholars in explaining human behavior particularly in respect of group and social relations. It would appear that in order to justify the agonic mode, we are willing to forget our hedonic heritage.

While we generally agree with Morgan, we also believe that civilizations differ in the relative emphasis that they place on these two modes. Both modes are present in every civilization, but the relative emphasis varies. In our understanding, the Indian civilization leans more towards the hedonic mode. In order to pursue this line of thought, we have compared and contrasted the two modes in Table 8.3.

As we look at the main elements of this table and relate them to the features mentioned in the chapter on Indianness, as well as the EUM findings, it becomes reasonably clear that our civilizational tilt is towards the hedonic mode.

Prestige has been and continues to be of greater importance to Indians than *Power*. A potential loss of face, or the prospect of being "shamed" is a source of great anxiety to many Indians. Given

Table 8.3 Comparing the agonic and the hedonic modes of centripetal collectives

The Agonic Mode	The Hedonic Mode
The group is seen as a source of common defense to an external threat.	The group is seen as a source of dependence and mutual confidence.
The group is organized around an individual who has the greatest *fighting* ability and maximum resource holding potential.	The group is organized around an individual who has the maximum *prestige* – prestige comes from altruistic acts or superior skills.
The intragroup relations are marked by mutual defensiveness and the group develops ways and means to ensure that the hostilities within the group are *controlled* and *contained*.	Intragroup behavior is governed by signals of mutual *assurance* and *support*.
This is achieved through a rigid pecking order, compliance and threat of punishment.	Physical proximity, touch and sharing are encouraged whereas defensive behavior is deactivated.
The bonding between members is in the nature of an alliance against a potential enemy.	The bonding within the group is built through an exploration of the social environment and a sense of play.
All relationships are determined by dominance and submission.	There is no major preoccupation with threat from within the group.

the low USD score in SC and much higher in OP, inviting defensive attention to oneself, cannot be a very pleasant prospect. Hence diffusing or deflecting any potential hostility becomes a major preoccupation. In the strength–skill divide, there is a clear preference for skill. It is the skilled archer Arjuna who is regarded as the ultimate hero and not the stronger mace warrior Bhīma. References to the famous Indian rope trick are legendary. It is perhaps no coincidence that India has produced many more spin wizards than tear-away fast bowlers in cricket. The Indian domination in the field of hockey was always based on skillful maneuvering of the ball rather than speed and strength.

As we saw in case of Ravi, the authority relationships in the Indian tradition have been configured around *"reverence in exchange of being taken care of (the mai baap phenomenon)"* rather than antagonism. There are very few instances of patricide in Indian history. Simultaneously there is no clear linkage between hierarchy and privilege/consumption.

The Gandhian historian Dharampal[8] in his research on 18th- and 19th-century India found out that there were no marked differences in the consumption patterns of the rich and the poor.

In fact, it was a matter of great concern to our colonial masters that the rich folk in India "squandered" their money on wasteful activities like temple donations. According to Dharampal, what the British were doing to Indians was no worse than what they did to their own underprivileged. The essential issue is not just racial but also the meanings associated with power relationships. In the agonic mode, power is an entitlement to oppress and exploit. In the hedonic mode, power is a responsibility to look after the less powerful.

We also find great comfort in Indians with physical proximity and sharing. It is not uncommon for Indians to share food with complete strangers during a train journey. In fact, many people will find it rude to eat themselves without offering it to the other. Often people from other cultures find the high physical contact between Indian men somewhat strange. In India, people easily narrate their personal and family stories to complete strangers whom they may meet on the road or the marketplace or on a train journey. Unlike the modern gated communities and shopping malls, a highly personalized connect with your neighbors and shopkeepers, as well as others, was the norm.

Simultaneously, Indians have had great difficulty in uniting against a common enemy, an essential feature of the agonic mode. Thus, it is not surprising that historical humiliations suffered at the hands of external aggressors often become clarion calls for creating a baboon-like hegemonic society that is based on the agonic mode.

Ironically in this process, the basic positive strengths of the hedonic mode are forgotten. As Michael Chance points out, it is the hedonic mode that propels human creative intelligence. It enhances the attentional capacity of the individual and makes it more open and flexible, allowing different inputs to be integrated.

The much-cherished Indian strengths of resilience, inclusivity and ingenuity are directly linked to the hedonic mode. However, there seems to be an increasing pressure to tilt more towards the agonic mode, creating considerable stress at the psychic level and strife at the social level.

We find the same stress reflected in the EUM data of our respondents. Simply put, what they seem to be saying is "My inclination is towards the hedonic mode, but I find myself in a world which operates in the agonic mode, and hence the best I can do to survive and prosper is to modify myself and embrace the agonic mode".

This stance makes integration of the two modes very difficult. The agonic mode is denied in the Self, and the hedonic mode is denied in the context. In such a situation, the individual can neither be "self-reliant" nor "depend on others".

Integrating the three strands

Figure 8.1 offers a depiction of two perspectives that get created given the three strands that have been referred to in the preceding chapters. These two perspectives are being defined as P1 and P2.

The three strands explored in this chapter do not operate in isolation but are intimately connected with each other. The Homo economicus, Rational Ingenieur, and the agonic mode have a highly synergistic relationship and thus reinforce each other. Together, they constitute what we have called the first or Hema's perspective (P1), which flows from a large part of current management paradigms.

On the other side, Homo reciprocans, Bricoleur and the hedonic mode tend to hang together, and we refer to them as P2, which is the perspective that people like Ravi hold and is derived essentially from Indian civilizational codings.

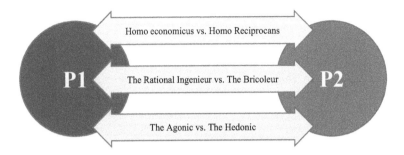

Homo economicus vs. Homo Reciprocans

P1

The Rational Ingenieur vs. The Bricoleur

P2

The Agonic vs. The Hedonic

Figure 8.1 Depiction of two perspectives

Each of these perspectives represents a significant human imperative. These two imperatives seem mutually exclusive and contradictory to each other but, in fact, complement each other. Neither perspective can stand without the other and needs the counter-pull of the other for its own existence.

P1 represents the human imperative of existential aloneness. Each one of us comes into this world alone and will depart alone. Each of us must take responsibility for our own fate and destiny. Each of us tries to gain mastery over our life and life conditions through mustering all our resources – rationality being the most significant of our resources. In the ultimate analysis, we cannot depend on anyone else. Furthermore, in some sense, all other beings (human or parts of nature) are objects of utility for us and have very little significance otherwise. Thus, it is only natural that each of us is guided by self-interest, that each of us tries to maximize his or her influence on others, that each of us tries to keep control through clear road maps of where we wish to go and how and that each of us must watch against the prospect of being exploited by others.

In the EUM framework, this perspective belongs to the right side of the spiral, that is, USD and UPA (see Figure 3.1).

On the other side is the imperative of existential connectedness, which is held by P2. Each of us is born into a context and will leave behind a context. No matter how significant we may believe ourselves to be, in the larger scheme of things, we are nothing beyond a small drop in the ever -flowing river of life. No matter how hard we may try, we can never be self-sufficient and will always remain dependent on other human beings and uncertainties of nature and life forces. Looked from this angle, it only makes sense that we learn to place greater emphasis on the interest of the collective over our own self-interest; learn to share with others and hold them with love, caring and respect; learn to go along with the flow of life; and learn to surrender ourselves to the larger forces that govern human existence.

In the EUM framework this perspective belongs to the left side of the spiral, that is, UBP, URB and UMI (see Figure 3.1).

Every civilization tries to co-hold/balance these imperatives but inevitably leans a little more on one side or the other. Insights from different scholars, our own experience and EUM data show that our civilizational predisposition is towards P2 and that the prevalent paradigms in the corporate world are derived from P1. It is this incongruence that is at the heart of the difficulty that the Indian managers face in their attempt to manage the leadership polarities mentioned in the previous chapter. In our understanding, the meanings and significances associated with the eight elements of the four polarities are quite different in the two perspectives.

Preservation versus transformation

Preservation in P1 is associated with being closed, unwillingness to let go what one has, stagnation and so on. In P2, preservation is associated with contentment, valuing of one's heritage and acceptance of limitations, among other attributes. Similarly, transformation in P1 is associated with adventure, volition, agency and shaping of the context in accordance with a preset design. It will be akin to sculpting whereby a piece of rock is transformed into a beautiful statue. In contrast, transformation in P2 will be associated with natural unfolding of inherent potential – it will be akin to gardening whereby a seed is nourished and fostered into becoming a plant or a robust tree. The two approaches fundamentally alter the relationship between the old and the new. In P1, the old is either discarded in favor of the new or acted on and made new, whereas in the P2, the old is looked after and facilitated to renew itself.

Meritocracy versus humanism

In P1, merit is defined primarily in terms of success and achievement. As the Hindi saying goes, "*Jo jeeta wahi Sikander*" (Nothing succeeds like success!). On the other hand, in P2, merit is defined in terms of devotion to one's task, quality of endeavor and commitment to the system. Similarly, humanism in P1 rests on notions such as fairness, transparency and equal opportunity, whereas in P2, humanism rests on notions of sympathy, care and compassion. The tension between meritocracy and humanism in the P1 is sought to be resolved through the principle of "fair reward /compensation commensurate with contribution". On the other hand, in P2, the operative principle becomes "from each according to ability and to each according to need".

Control versus empowerment

In P1, control is exercised through structural/legal provisions and requires external enforcement. The attempt is to discipline through punitive action/motivational rewards to ensure that everything is moving as per plan. In P2, control is exercised through social approval/disapproval, and hence, the reliance is on self-regulation and restraint to ensure that the system operates harmoniously. Empowerment in P1 pertains to legitimate structural authority and ability to exercise it in a responsible manner. In P2, empowerment is derived from systemic commitment and mutual reassurance. Thus, the operative principle in the P1 is "authority commensurate with responsibility", but the operative principle in P2 is "building trust and mutual confidence".

Objective rationality versus subjective wisdom

In P1, truth is absolute, and objective rationality is the pathway to it. Subjectivity is seen as dangerous because it is influenced by self-interest and personal prejudices. The preference is to eliminate subjectivity to the extent possible and/or vest it in the hands of a select few in the form of discretion for dealing with exceptional situations with sufficient checks and balances. In P2, Truth is multiple and contextual. The so-called objective rationality, in fact, is a product of subjective predispositions and preferred ways of looking at any phenomenon. Thus, while in the P1 difference of opinion is engaged through rational discussion and debate, in P2, such differences can only be addressed through self-reflection, empathetic listening and process of dialog.

Table 8.4 gives the main features of the four leadership polarities as seen through the two perspectives.

Table 8.4 Leadership implications of the two perspectives

	P1 ERA Leadership	P2 RBH Leadership
Preservation versus Transformation	Preservation is seen as being unwilling to change and associated with stagnation. Transformation is seen as an adventure that is agentic and emphasizes the need to act on. Legacy and the old are to be discarded or acted on in favor of newness.	Preservation is seen with contentment, and limitations are seen as but natural. Transformation is a process that is seen as natural unfolding and evolutionary. Legacy and the old are to be looked after, and newness is seen as a renewal process.
Meritocracy versus Humanism	Merit is defined in terms of ability to succeed and competencies/knowledge. Humanism is defined in terms of transparency, fairness and equal opportunities. The tension between the two is resolved through commensurate rewards for contribution.	Merit is defined in terms of 'devotion' to the task and commitment to the system. Humanism is seen in terms of care, sympathy and compassion. The tension between the two is resolved through "from each according to ability and to each according to need".
Control versus Empowerment	Control is exercised through structure/law and punitive action through external enforcement – towards achieving the plan. Empowerment is endorsed through legitimization of structural authority and responsible role taking. The tension between the two is worked through by defining authority vis-à-vis responsibility	Control is exercised through social approval/disapproval leading to self-regulation – all this towards harmony within the system. Empowerment is endorsed through commitment and mutual reassurance. The tension between the two processes is worked with by building trust and mutual confidence.

(Continued)

Table 8.4 (Continued)

	P1 ERA Leadership	P2 RBH Leadership
Objective Rationality versus Subjective Wisdom	Truth is absolute and objective. Subjectivity is dangerous as it is governed by prejudice and self-interest. Subjectivity is to be eliminated or to be vested with chosen few. The tension is managed through rational discussions and debate.	Truth is multiple and contextual. Objective rationality is just one of the lens of looking at phenomena – the others are 'intuition', 'gut-feel' and so on. The tension between the two is managed through self-reflection and deep dialog.

The main difficulty of the Indian managers, in engaging with these polarities, stems from their unease with both P1 and P2 centric meanings. Their training and understanding of the management paradigms propel them to the P1 centric meanings, but their civilizational predisposition does not allow them to embrace them fully.

Simultaneously, they believe that while their P2 leaning may be fine in their social and family life, it has no place in the corporate world. In their role as managers, they keep oscillating between the two sets of meanings. For example, the P1-centric meaning of humanism that relies on candor and transparency is paid lip service to, but their actual engagements with people are often determined by P2-centric concern for feelings of other people. This ambivalence often makes it very difficult for them to operate with any conviction.

Simultaneously, we believe this unease with the two sets is also their biggest resource. It opens the possibility of acknowledging the importance of both perspectives and integrating them. However, such integration will require significant shifts both at the individual level and the systemic level. In the last chapter, we outline our understanding of what these shifts might entail.

Notes

1 Mill, J. S. (1836). *Essays on Some Unsettled Questions of Political Economy* (Second Edition ed., Vol. Essay 5). London: Longmans, Green, Reader & Dyer.

2 Jajmani or Yajmani System is the traditional system based on the exchange of goods and services between land-owning higher castes and landless service castes. The service castes traditionally include weavers, leatherworkers, blacksmiths, goldsmiths, barbers and washermen and so constitute groups of artisans serving the community. The landed higher-caste *Jajman* are the patrons, and the service castes are the *kameen* (servers) of the *Jajman*. The Jajmani system is based on the agricultural system of production and distribution of goods and services. It is the link between the land-owning high-caste groups and occupational castes.

3 Strauss, C. L. (1962). *The Savage Mind* (G. W. Nicholson, Trans.). Paris: University of Chicago Press.

4 *The Dabbawala System: On-Time Delivery Every Time*, Harvard Business School Case 610 059 (February 2010).

5 Chance, M. R. (1988). *Social Fabrics of the Mind*. London: Psychology Press and Taylor & Francis Group.

6 Morgan, E. (2009). *The Aquatic Ape Hypothesis*. Souvenir Press.

7 Devore, I. (1965). *Primate Behavior: Field Studies of Monkeys and Apes*. Canada: Holt, Rinehart & Winston of Canada Limited.

8 Dharampal. (2003). *Rediscovering India*. SIDH.

Chapter 9

Integrating the two perspectives

As we reflect on what we see of the Indian manager, we are filled with both a sense of celebration and some sadness. There is much to celebrate in the gifts which the Indian manager brings – flexibility, tenacity, resilience, ingenuity, ability to negotiate through the complex network of relationships and, last but not the least, commitment to the system. Sadly, often these gifts are deployed in coping with the emergent situation rather than taking charge and proactively shaping it.

Perhaps, the main reason for this is that a large part of the individual's energy and effort gets expended in balancing the tension generated by the two perspectives explicated in the previous chapter. The first perspective (P1) propels him or her towards individualism, a need to be on top of the situation and being perpetually battle-ready. On the other hand, the second perspective (P2) pulls the individual towards concern for relationships, going with the flow and a need for an amiable and warm interface with the world.

In the previous chapter, Table 8.4 highlights this tension through the leadership lens.

Many Indian managers are able to integrate the two perspectives and achieve phenomenal results. However, many others are unable to do so and hence find it difficult to provide space for their inner creativity to flourish and find expression. They find themselves juggling through these opposing forces and somehow keeping their heads above water. This does not impair their managerial efficacy but seriously damages their leadership potential, as it becomes difficult for them to act from conviction and legitimize/authorize themselves to act on behalf of the system. Thus, we often find that the same manager who can act firmly and decisively in respect of his or her own area of responsibility becomes extremely tentative when invited to expand his or her area of influence and impact the larger context. The key to unlocking the potential of the Indian manager lies in the ability to co-hold the two perspectives. We also believe that the need for this co-holding is not just applicable to Indian managers but has a much larger applicability. While humanity has progressed and benefited considerably from P1 (particularly post-industrialization), its limitations and downsides are becoming far too obvious in the postmodern era.

In this respect, the Indian managers have a distinct advantage. Their heritage has gifted them a natural inclination towards P2. If, instead of holding this heritage in shame and doubt, they were to embrace it, they could well become the torchbearers of an approach, which is better suited not just to the Indian context but also to the larger global scheme of things.

For this to happen, we will need to reconfigure the relationship between the "Indian civilizational predispositions" and the "imperatives of living", in our times, particularly in respect of the corporate world. This reconfiguration has implications both at the individual level as well as at the system level. While there are no easy readymade answers, what we offer in the following is our understanding of this reconfiguration both at the individual and systemic levels.

Reconfiguration and its implications at the individual level

Exercising responsible agency

Co-holding of P1 and P2 presumes the exercising of responsible agency by the individual, that is, acting both for oneself and for the larger context. The seeds of agency are sown in the USD, and the responsibility associated with them is learned in later Universes, that is, URB, UPA and UMI. If the lessons of USD are not adequately learned and internalized, the entire structure of responsible agency remains fragile. In such a scenario, the later Universes become burdensome and oppressive.

As the EUM data show, the Universe that is most problematic for our respondents is USD. It is repressed in oneself and projected onto others. Thus, exercising responsible agency does not come easily to Indian managers. Often, they get caught in what was earlier described as the "puppet or a loose cannon" syndrome, that is, either disowning all volition and getting completely controlled by the situation OR acting in an arbitrary and reckless manner with no concern for the impact on others.

The following are the four main hurdles that Indian managers face in exercising *responsible agency*:

a   *Managing aggressive impulses*

Given the taboo on aggression in the Indian tradition, it is not surprising that most Indians find it difficult to manage their aggressive impulses. These are either suppressed or projected on to others or discharged indiscriminately. Consequently, both agonic and hedonic modes become problematic. Even in the agonic mode, aggressive impulses need to be controlled and managed.

As Michael Chance has observed, in the highly agonic baboon society, it is the baboon who controls and manages his aggressive impulses better that makes it to the top, not the baboon who is most aggressive. On the other hand, in the hedonic mode, the "other" has to be seen as "non-threatening". This is clearly not the case for Indian managers as indicated by the high OP score in USD. No exercise of responsible agency is feasible in such a scenario, for one would either be constantly curbing one's own aggressive impulses or constantly watching one's back.

b   *Differentiating between authority and hierarchy*

As mentioned in the chapter on Indianness, the notion of authority gets intertwined with the notion of hierarchy to the extent that the two become indistinguishable. It is presumed that authority can only be exercised by a person of higher hierarchical status vis-à-vis a person who is lower to him or her in the pecking order. Thus, authority as a structural arrangement for task performance becomes compromised. Situations in which a person of a lower rank has to exercise authority over a person of higher rank (e.g., a lowly audit assistant vis-à-vis a powerful departmental head) become challenging. In such a scenario, the exercising of responsible agency is severely undermined by apprehensions of disturbing the hierarchical balance.

c   *Affirming oneself*
For many Indians, growing out of the psychological son/daughter role is not very easy. Filial devotion is considered as one of the highest virtues with very little space for antagonism or hostility in authority relationships. The primacy given to the belonging system also makes the individual hypersensitive to what others think and feel about him or her. Therefore, the individual is constantly seeking affirmation and approval from others, particularly significant authority figures. In such a situation, the individual can only feel legitimate in exercising agency when he or she believes that he or she is acting on behalf of the system and enjoys the support of significant others.

d   *Preoccupation with purity and pollution*
We suspect that many Indians tend to bifurcate their needs and desires as "pure" and "impure". Given the emphasis on selflessness and renunciation, there is considerable squeamishness around self-centric needs such as status, recognition, centrality and the like. They are either pursued under the garb of more exalted needs, such as concern for others, contributing to team/organization performance and so on, or suppressed. Simultaneously these needs which are held as "dirty and lower level" are projected on to others. Thus, competitiveness often degenerates into sibling rivalry, jealousy and undermining of the "other".

Sometimes there is also a counterreaction in the form of an "I am entitled to pursue all my needs in any way that I feel like without any care for consequences for others/larger context". In such cases agency gets degenerated into "meri marzi" (as I wish) phenomenon.

We therefore believe that exercising responsible agency will entail considerable investment in the following areas:

• Acknowledging and managing aggressive impulses
• Learning to differentiate between authority and hierarchy

- Affirming and legitimizing oneself
- Acknowledging all one's needs/desires, gracing them and pursuing them in a responsible manner

Working with differences

The second set of issues that Indian managers need to address pertain to handling differences. Our experience, as well as the EUM data, suggests that Indian managers have a remarkable ability to "live" with differences. However, this ability rarely gets translated into "working" with differences in a way that the differences can become a resource for oneself and the system. In order to explicate this, it will be helpful to recall what had been stated earlier about the Indian ways of engaging with differences.

If the Indian managers wish to co-hold the two perspectives, they will need to go beyond these coping strategies and discover ways of harnessing the creative and transformative potential of differences. Some of the major hurdles that they face in this endeavor are as follows:

a   *Conflict avoidance*
    Given their low USD orientation, Indian managers generally like to stay away from direct combat. Their preferred ways are adjustment, sidestepping, compromise or deployment of indirect/insidious strategies. Therefore, quite often there is a considerable gap between the stated position of the person and his or her real thoughts and feelings. Needless to say, this is not an ideal scenario for meaningful dialog and exploring the creative potential of differences.

b   *Narrowly defined personal responsibility*
    Most Indians have a strong sense of responsibility towards their own system of belonging. This could be their family, their circle of friends or their work group. However, it rarely extends to the larger system with which they do not have a personal connection. In respect of the larger system, their attitude is either of indifference or of an external critic who comments as an outside observer. Therefore, on systemic issues either the differences remain unexpressed or are engaged with only from the perspective of one's own subsystem. Engagement with

differences from a total system perspective becomes extremely difficult. Often, functions with integrative responsibility (e.g., HR) are required to engage with each subsystem separately and address their concern. The consequence of such a process is that the total system responsibility remains either with the concerned integrative function or at the very top, and rarely becomes a shared agenda.

c *Security through relationships*
The primary source of security for most Indian managers is the network of their relationships rather than their competence and/or contribution. Often, there is very little relationship between the competence/contribution of an Indian manager and his or her sense of security. Even highly competent managers start feeling insecure if anything goes wrong in their relationships particularly with significant others. Consequently, many Indian managers prefer to remain within the comfort zone of familiarity and are generally averse to taking interpersonal risk. This obviously restricts their experimentation with any idea/perspective that is a significant departure from what their reference group is accustomed to.

d *Role and structural ambiguities*
Role and structure are the main anchors of stability for the Indian manager. Consequently, any ambiguity in these becomes stressful for the individual to handle. Most Indian managers like to clearly understand as to what is their area of influence and what are the boundaries in which they must operate. Once this clarity is achieved, they seek complete control over their delineated territory. Not surprisingly, many traditional Indian companies operated (and still do) as a collation of clans run by reasonably autonomous and authoritarian satraps. In this arrangement, there was very little need to work with differences. The intra-territory differences could be handled by the concerned satrap, and there was a tacit understanding among satraps that they will not interfere into each other's territory. With increasing complexity and gradual shifts in power relationships, the older arrangements are under considerable stress, and the new structures require a more direct engagement with a wide range of differences that cut across traditional

boundaries of functions, locations, hierarchical status and like. Needless to say, dealing with these multilayered and multi-nuanced differences requires a much greater comfort with role and structural ambiguities than many Indian managers are able to muster.

We believe that the traditional approaches of Indian managers in dealing with differences are unlikely to work in times to come. The Indian managers will need to learn more direct ways of engaging with differences if they wish to harness their creative and trans-formative potential. This will need investment in the following:

a Direct engagement with conflict
b Expanding the scope of engagement to larger systemic issues
c Reducing dependence on relationships, and
d Getting comfortable with structural/role ambiguities.

Table 9.1 summarizes the challenges as well as new choices that the Indian manager may like to explore at an individual level.

Reconfiguration and its implications at the systemic level

The co-holding of P1 and P2 cannot be accomplished only through interventions at the individual level. Unless the context provides facilitative conditions, the individual, no matter how hard he or she tries, will not be able to accomplish this co-holding. The ground conditions will need to integrate both the civilizational predisposi-tions of the Indian psyche and imperatives of living in the present-day world, particularly with respect to the corporate sector. Some of the significant features of this, in our opinion, are as follows:

1 Centrality of Dharma
    If the Indian way of living was to be described in a single word, it would surely be Dharma. *Dharma* is an interesting word as it has two distinct sets of meanings. One set of mean-ings has a normative flavor – it is built around the theme of "righteous conduct", that is, the 'oughts' and 'shoulds', the ethical and moral codes, the appropriate social conduct and the like. Simultaneously, the word *Dharma* also connotes "innate-ness" (e.g., it is the Dharma of earth to go around the sun). In this set, Dharma is not just a normative construct but also a

Table 9.1 Shifts needed at the individual level

Areas to Be Aware Of	Experienced Difficulties at Individual Levels	What to Invest In
Exercising responsible agency	Aggressive impulses are seen as taboo and are either repressed or projected on to the Other – may manifest in passive-aggressive behavior.	Acknowledgment of one's own aggressive impulses Contain and manage one's own impulses Seeing aggression as a natural human phenomenon and not holding the other responsible for it Expressing it in a responsible manner, without being destructive.
	Inability to exercise lateral and upwards authority	Learning to differentiate between authority and hierarchy would enable the individual to overcome the challenge
	Growing out of the psychological son/ daughter role is extremely difficult, and thus, there is a continuous need for affirmation from others in work systems.	Affirming and legitimizing oneself is key to one's maturation as an individual. Seeing others as human beings as opposed to symbols of relationship Differentiating UMI from UBP in the EUM framework can facilitate this shift.
	Preoccupation with purity and pollution emphasizes on exalted, values and 'altruistic behavior' (for the sake of others/systems) and a denial of self-centric behaviors that are labeled as dirty or low level.	Acknowledging all ones needs/ desires, gracing them and pursuing them in a responsible manner. Differentiating the two Universes of URB and UDS offers a way out of compulsion to behave in status appropriate ways.

(Continued)

Table 9.1 (Continued)

Areas to Be Aware Of	Experienced Difficulties at Individual Levels	What to Invest In
Working with differences	There is a propensity to see conflict as scary, and a need for avoiding it. This comes from low identification with USD and projecting it on to others.	To own up the USD in oneself and recognize the creative potential of conflict
	Narrowly defined personal responsibility that allows the Indian manager to insulate him- or herself from the demands of the larger system and its inherent complexity and diversity.	Dissolving the fear of apprehended backlash through experimenting and dialog would enable the individual to engage with systemic issues.
	There is an apprehension about stepping on others territory that reinforces this mind-set.	Dissolving the myth of non-negotiability in systems is critical for working with differences.
	Security through relationships does not allow working with differences and diversity within the system – thus, all differences are either swept beneath the carpet or escalated.	Investment is required to get out of the seduction of amiability and discovering new relatedness.
	Overreliance on clarity of expectations	Getting comfortable with non-affiliative relationships in task systems
		Getting comfortable with shared ownership of the task and the context
		Dissolving the fear of potential accusations

statement of the true essence of something or the existential imperatives associated with it.

The fusion of the normative with existential imperatives, has significant implications for human striving. In the Indian scheme of things, all striving has to be in consonance with the intrinsic essence. If striving is violative of the existential imperatives or an oppressive imposition, then it will be regarded as Adharmic. This striving could be in the area of human exchange or in interface with nature or other forms of life, the basic principle of nonviolent striving will apply.

In sharp contrast to this, striving in P1 is associated with gaining mastery over one's context and shaping it in accordance with one's will. In this scenario, any potential violation of "innateness" will be treated as a collateral damage and/or price to be paid for achieving what one desires. Striving here is governed by the desired impact/end state that one wants, and the "innateness" is only a resource to be deployed or a hurdle to be crossed.

Since the current paradigms of management theory and practice are based on a P1 kind of striving, several difficulties arise in relating them to the notion of Dharma. Some of the main ones are as follows:

a   A large part of prevalent management paradigms is built around the primacy of goals, outcomes and consequences. It is assumed that all striving is triggered by a desire to accomplish certain goals, and the clearer one is about both the goals and focused on the path to achieve them, the greater will be the chances of success. Thus, there is considerable emphasis on constructs like goal setting, goal-directed movement, cost–benefit analysis, bottom-line and quarter-to-quarter results and the like. Clearly, there is very little space for notions such as Nishkaama Karma, that is, operating from one's convictions and accepting the consequences as they emerge. Similarly, any choice/action which is detrimental to one's self-interest will be considered foolhardy, except in such cases where a "short-term loss" is considered necessary for a "long-term gain".

b   Another difficulty arises from the importance attached to growth and size. It would be a rare organization that does not worship the deity of growth. Becoming the largest/most dominant and/or growing at an exponential rate usually figure quite prominently in the scheme of things, of most organizations. In contrast, in the Dharmic mode, striving has to be directed towards wholesomeness rather than growth in size. The striving has to be respectful of the innateness and allow its natural potential to unfold rather than imposing a predetermined end state. It is believed that such imposition, even if successful, will only create cancerous growth and generate toxicity. It is not surprising therefore that many traditional Indian businesses show ambivalence towards growth and chose not to go beyond the "boutique size", particularly if they take pride in their quality or are selective about their clients. However, in the present context, it is becoming extremely difficult for them to do so. The message from the macro-context seems loud and clear: "Grow or Perish".

c   In the Dharmic mode all relationships are governed by the notion of *Maryada*, that is, respect for each other's innateness and boundaries. This applies to relationships between individuals, between subsystems and between the total system and its environment. Even conflict situations such as wars have to be engaged within the frame of Maryada. Clearly there is no room for notions such as "all is fair in love and war". This is equally applicable to nonconflictual relationships like that with the customer. In the Dharmic mode, the customer is neither treated like a "king" nor an "imbecile sucker" but as a "partner" in an exchange that is governed by mutual respect and dignity.

This is a very different perspective than what is prevalent in the current management paradigms. A large part of management theory and practice is based on the principle of effectiveness in relationships. This effectiveness is sought to be achieved either through dominance or through forging mutually beneficial links. Not surprisingly, the term *win–win* is one of the most commonly used expressions for an effective relationship. On the face of it, it seems like *Maryada* but has a very different flavor. It is often characterized by subtle indignities and collusive alliances. The principle of win–win allows the concerned parties to arrive at a mutually beneficial arrangement, but more often than not, the price for this collusion is borne by an unsuspecting third party (e.g., customer, another subsystem, etc.) or the larger environment.

> The current ecological crisis being faced by the world is a stark example of the unintended consequences of win–win relationships forged in the name of "all round development".

Clearly, it is not very easy to accommodate the imperatives arising from the prevalent management paradigms with the Dharmic mode. Some steps that we believe can help in this endeavor are the following:

- Place equal (if not more) emphasis on process, systemic commitment and institutional contribution rather than achievement of targets, bottom lines and so on.
- Focus attention on wholesomeness and proportion and not just growth and size.
- Encourage people to act from "conviction" rather than "consequences"
- Review relationships not just for effectiveness but also for mutual respect and dignity.

2 Psychological ownership and empowerment

As has been stated earlier Indians have a strong commitment to their system of belonging. However, this commitment is often restricted to the immediate system with which they have a personalized connect. When it comes to engaging with the larger system with which they have no personalized connect, the situation takes a 180-degree turn. In such situations, the relationship is often characterized by indifference and even extraction, that is, negative reciprocity. The system then becomes a depersonalized entity from which one can extract to the maximum extent without any care for its well-being and replenishment. This is a major hurdle that almost all start-ups face when they transition from a small, close group to a large, formal setup.

Thus, forging an emotive connect between the individual and the organization is of critical importance in the Indian context. To some extent, in the more traditional organizations, this emotive connect was forged by longevity of association. However, over time, particularly in last couple of decades, the situation has changed considerably.

As is often said, in present times people don't join an organization to build a career. Instead, they join assignments that they believe fit into their scheme of things. In a sense, the individual has reclaimed his or her responsibility for building a career for him- or herself and is no longer willing to restrict his or her horizon to any one organization. This has left a vacuum for the organizations, and they are wondering as to how to make themselves more attractive to the individual and how to enhance the stickiness factor.

However, most of these attempts are anchored in P1 and disregard P2. Some of the main difficulties that arise are as follows:

a   Relationships in P1 are determined either by relative power of the concerned parties or by mutual need gratification. In the good old days, the balance of power was clearly in favor of the organization, which is no longer the case. Thus, it is not surprising that in many organizations the individual is treated not like a "member" but like an "external entity", and the endeavor is to provide a rewarding experience to him or her. There is very little difference between the way organizations treat their Employee Engagement Surveys and the way they treat their Customer Satisfaction Surveys. It is not uncommon for organizations to have targets for Employee Engagement Scores for individual managers. We have often experienced leadership teams in organizations behave like anxious parents who are constantly worrying about whether they are doing "enough" for their "children" and whether the "children" are performing as well as they should. It is a rare organization that treats its people who are "members" with a systemic stake and who are both a part of the "problem" and part of the "solution".

Not surprisingly, for his or her part, the employee also looks at the organization as a "customer" who is "buying" the skills/competencies/output/time of the individual for a certain price. This basic paradigm is deployed in virtually all relationships. The term *internal customer* is not just freely used but is also seen as a sign of professionalism. Clearly there is little scope for emotive connect and psychological ownership in this scenario.

b   Another feature that impacts empowerment is the apprehension with which most organizations look at subjectivity. In P1, it is assumed that subjectivity will be governed by self-interest and prejudices of the individual who is exercising it. Thus, most organizations either try to eliminate it or put in sufficient checks and balances to ensure that it is exercised prudently. While to an extent, this is necessary to ensure a degree of fairness in the system, it also alienates the individual from the organization. It is well-nigh impossible for any individual to emotionally invest in a space where there is no room for his or her feelings, predispositions and preferences. The end result is that either the individual finds surreptitious ways of subjective expression or emotionally withdraws from the system and settles for a dry, transactional relationship.

The impact of this phenomenon becomes visible in the way attempts at strengthening the bond between the individual and the organization are received. In our experience interventions like mission/vision/value statements and town-hall meetings that are undertaken for this purpose become dry, mechanical exercises and often even evoke cynicism. Very rarely have we seen them having the impact that they are intended to have.

c   Another difficulty arises from the posturing that P1 demands. As per the dictates of posturing, the individual has to put his or her best foot forward, always appear confident and never show any vulnerability. Every encounter becomes a performance and often a contest for centrality and being one-up. In most organizations we find, there is far too much of discussion and debate and very little dialog. Debate is a win–lose exercise in which one tries to convince the other of one's point of view through rational argument. On the other hand, a dialog requires sharing of not just facts and reasons but also the feelings, beliefs and assumptions that underpin the thoughts and ideas that are being articulated. Simultaneously, a dialog requires empathetic listening and an understanding not just at a rational level but also an appreciation of the hopes, fears, anxieties and preferences that are influencing the stances of the other person.

In this scenario, it is to be expected that each person feels alone and believes that there is no one whom he or she can count on for understanding, let alone support. While it is difficult for anyone to feel empowered in this setting, the issue is particularly acute in the Indian context. As stated earlier, in the Indian psyche, empowerment is less determined by structural arrangements, such as delegation of authority, and more by the ambience of relationships that surround the individual. To that extent, it becomes even more difficult for the Indian managers to empower themselves.

Empowerment, psychological ownership and emotive connect are intimately linked in the Indian psyche. Some specific shifts that may be of help in this regard are as follows:

- Exercises such as Employee Engagement Surveys should be undertaken for understanding the quality of the relationship between the individual and the organization rather than as a quantitative/normative measure of organization's attractiveness to the individual.
- Instead of formal presentations and discussion forums, there should be an investment in informal settings for sharing of thoughts and feelings and fostering dialog.
- There should be much more deployment of symbols, folklore, stories, myths for forging a link with the larger system rather than mission/vision/value statements and formal town-hall meetings.
- Work groups should meet periodically to share how people are feeling both with themselves and with each other – their hopes,

fears, frustrations, anxieties, satisfactions and so on – primarily with the view of building empathetic understanding and clearing the air.

• Proactive investment in building the capability of their leaders to exercise subjective wisdom in a responsible manner rather than relying exclusively on objective rationality.

3 Androgyny and management

The prevalent management thinking and practice is primarily based on the masculine principle, either static or dynamic. Thus, notions of power are derived primarily from the dynamic masculine principle and rest on features such as assertion, impact and dominance. The dynamic feminine features of power, such as evocation, creative expression, intuition and a magnetic pull among others, receive much less attention. Similarly, notions of fairness and justice are derived from the static masculine principle viz. reasonableness and uniform application of rules and regulations. The static feminine notions of justice that are more based on care, compassion and sensitivity are rarely taken into account. Thus, while many more women are being welcomed into the corporate world, there are very few organizations who have opened their doors to femininity.

> As stated earlier, the Indian psyche leans towards the feminine/androgynous. The near-exclusive emphasis on the masculine principle in the prevalent management paradigms places the Indian manager in a difficult situation. The individual has to constantly be vigilant about his or her own feminine features and often regards them (as shown by our data) as a liability to be overcome. The feminine side is either completely repressed with a display of exaggerated masculinity or held in shame and doubt.

We believe that gracing of the feminine will go a long way in enabling the Indian managers to act from conviction both for themselves as well as on behalf of the system. However, several difficulties stand in their way, some of the more significant ones being the following:

a   In most organizations, there is a marked preference for "prose like" expressions than "poetry like expressions". The main features of "prose like" expression are exactitude and clarity; hence, they are generally preplanned and close-ended. The more precise and clear the expression, the better. In contrast "poetry like" expressions are free-flowing and open-ended and carry multiple potential meanings. The recipient of a "poetry like" expression that includes narratives and sagas has to become an active participant in the meaning making process.

"Prose like" expressions are great for P1, which relies primarily on the static and dynamic masculine principles. The precision and clarity of "prose like" expressions enables uniformity of understanding and focused action. However, the dynamic feminine principle thrives on "poetry like" expressions and, hence, finds no room for itself in spaces that cannot withstand chaos, unpredictability and ambiguity. It is therefore no wonder that the feminine voice remains muted in most organizations.

b   In our experience, most organizations define their "competencies" in a highly masculine way. Communication skills generally emphasize the expressive dimension (articulation, cogency, assertiveness, persuasion, etc.) and underplay the receptive dimension (ability to listen, empathy, patience, etc.). Similarly, notions of Interpersonal competence center more around functionality than intimacy. It is a person who can achieve the desired results through collaboration of other people is regarded as being interpersonally effective, even if his or her relationships are devoid of any warmth and intimacy. Notions of openness are generally confined to candid sharing of information and ideas. They rarely encompass sharing of feelings and authentic human encounter. The fundamental assumption is that "feelings" of a person are his or her private affair and are not relevant/important in a task space.

Perhaps, this dominance of the masculine principle arises from a tight segregation between primary systems (spaces for belonging and affiliation) and secondary systems (spaces for task performance and achievement) As stated in Chapter 5, in the Indian psyche, there is a huge overlap between affiliative and task systems.

The basic picture of a task organization in the Indian mind is more of a human community than of an efficient impersonal machine. Consequently, exercises like competency mapping often appear theoretical and impractical to many Indian managers, they go along with them but invariably find ingenious ways of side-lining them.

The answer perhaps lies in recalibrating the competencies to the Indian context so that they become relevant to a frame where the basic emphasis is on looking at the organization as a community and where there is space for both masculine and feminine principles.

c Another difficulty arises from the way many organizations treat their support functions and infrastructure providers. We often come across scenarios where they are effectively treated as second-class citizens, akin to the way women are treated in a patriarchal society. Unless a function or a person is seen as directly contributing to the bottom line, its value remains dubious. The providers of support/infrastructure either resign to be the unsung heroes of the system or try to claim significance through other means. These other means include instituting complex centralized systems, which can be regarded as "professional" and/or reinventing themselves in the image of mainstream functions. Therefore, not surprisingly, many HR managers take greater pride and satisfaction from their "business partner" role than from their "employee champion" role.

This orientation toward support/infrastructure roles also impacts the perspectives on leadership, where the primary emphasis remains on "direction setting", "being decisive" and "leading from the front". While some lip service may be paid to notions such as "servant leader", there are very few leaders who are comfortable with being invisible and providing the infrastructure for others to take the center stage. More important, there are not many organizations who will regard these as "leadership qualities".

> We believe that simultaneity of the masculine and feminine principles holds the key to co-holding P1 and P2. This is particularly significant in the Indian context, given our androgynous predisposition.

In more specific terms, co-holding the masculine and the feminine will entail the following:

• Appreciation of open-ended, ambiguous expression that will provide space for the dynamic feminine to flourish
• Recalibrating the notions of managerial competencies to include both masculine and feminine perspectives
• Looking at organizations as purposive human communities and not just as efficient instruments of delivery
• Acknowledging the overlap between primary (affiliative) and secondary (task) systems rather than treating them as watertight compartments
• Gracing and valuing support/infrastructure functions and roles

Table 9.2 looks at the systemic perspective and summarizes new choices for the Indian manager

Concluding comments

We would like to conclude with an observation made by the historian Ramachandra Guha[1]: "*One might think of India as being Europe's past as well as its future*".

Guha's observation was made in a sociopolitical context, however, we believe that the same can be said about Indianness and the corporate world. On the face of it, many of the P2-centric traditional Indian ways of doing business seem outdated and out of tune with the present-day imperatives of the corporate world. However, they perhaps carry in them the seeds of things to come precisely because of this incongruence. In effect, they can provide a powerful counterpoint to the dominance of the P1 mode and thereby open newer possibilities of co-holding the two.

Management theorists worldwide have recognized a transformational shift in how human collectives are veering towards being acentric networks from erstwhile centripetal structures. Notions such as flexible terms, working from home, matrix organizations,

Table 9.2 Shifts needed at the organizational level

Themes	Present challenges	Significant shifts
Centrality of Dharma	Overemphasis on tangible results.	Emphasis on process and institutional contributions
	Overemphasis on relentless growth	Greater focus on wholesomeness and proportion
	Primary emphasis on transactional relationships that are mutually rewarding	Emphasis on mutual respect and dignity
Psychological ownership	Employee surveys taken as a quantitative or normative exercise (*Employees are treated either as customers or as children.*)	More emphasis on understanding the quality of the relationship between the individual and the organization (*Employees are responsible members within the system.*)
	Emphasis on formal presentations and discussions	Greater emphasis on sharing of thoughts and feelings and fostering dialog
	Primary reliance on objective rationality and enhancing analytical skills of people	Investing into subjective wisdom of the employees
Androgyny & management	Facts/logic-based closed-ended communication	Giving space to open-ended and symbolic narratives/expression
	Managerial leadership competencies defined in masculine terms	To encourage and offer greater space for feminine components of competencies
	More importance given to functions that have tangible outputs and show direct contribution to the bottom line	Gracing and valuing of support and infrastructure functions and roles

fluid relationships, frequent changes because of mergers and acqui-
sitions and so on have become fairly common already. It is reasonable to assume that organized systems of future in all spheres, work
or social, will not be built on the foundation of stable relationships.
This shift towards acentric networks is more threatening for P1.
Imagine an acentric network operating on the P1 foundation –
it will be sheer mayhem, with everyone scrambling to extract as
much as he or she can with no concern for replenishing the context.
Simultaneously, threat perceptions and paranoia will run high, and
the only source of safety/security that an individual will have is
through reliance on one's own resources and/or forging defensive
alliances against a common enemy. Turf wars and a never-ending
search for control mechanisms will become the order of the day.

In contrast, P2 has a much greater resonance with acentric networks. The hedonic mode with its emphasis on play and social relationships would create acentric networks where the primary pull
would be towards co-creating knowledge and new relatedness/reso-
nance with the "other" – where the "outsider" would be a guest
and not a threat. The Bricoleur's orientation towards surrender and
acceptance of limitation of resources will help in containing the
anxiety, which is inherent in an uncertain and fluid context. Similarly, the willingness to share and gift of the Homo reciprocans will
ensure that prestige is derived through acts of altruism rather than
from the dynamics of dominance and submission.

It is in this respect that we believe, Indian managers are in a
great position to co-hold the two perspectives. Their civilizational predisposition has taught them the imperatives of P2,
whereas their secondary socialization (schooling, professional
training, experience, etc.) teach them to deal with P1.

However, P2 by itself can also not meet the challenges of the emerging acentric networks. Without integrating P1, it will not be possible to deal with issues like task discipline, boundary management,
resource allocation, conflict resolution and the like. The human
reality includes both P1 and P2 propensities, and neither can be
overlooked.

As is evident from our data, our biggest difficulty comes from the
unease with which we hold our own civilizational predispositions.

We either glorify our heritage or treat it with disdain and as a burden. Perhaps we need to acknowledge that civilizational predispositions are neither a piece of clothing that can be discarded at will nor frozen molds of captivity. They always offer sufficient elbow room and degrees of freedom to reinterpret and recalibrate in the context of present times. However, in order to do this, we will first need to step out of normative frames of good/bad, right/wrong and so on and understand them for what they are. More important, this understanding has to come from our own perspective and not through borrowed frames and lenses.

For us, EUM is a modest step in trying to understand the Indian corporate reality through an Indian lens. Its Indianness does not stem from the fact that it has been developed by a group of Indians but from the fact that its basic philosophical foundations are Indian.

We would like to close with an extract from a talk delivered by Dr Sudhir &Kakar, at the University of Vienna in June 2017, where he dwelt upon Rabindranath Tagore's take on the relationship between Indianness and Western perspectives:

> Tagore believed that the future combination of the ideas of West and India could not come to fruition as long as the relationship between the two remained that of the giver and the receiver. A realization of the complementarity of the two ideas required that Indians first become aware of their heritage, of the spirit and mind of India, 'once upon a time we were in possession of such a thing as our own mind in India. It was living. It thought, it felt, it expressed itself'.

The wholesale acceptance of modern Western education has suppressed this mind. It has been treated like a wooden library shelf to be loaded volumes of secondhand information; 'In consequence it has lost its own color and character, and has borrowed polish from the carpenter's shop . . . we have bought our spectacles at the expense of our eyesight'.

Note

1 Guha, R. (2007). *India After Gandhi*. Picador India, p. 767.

For Product Safety Concerns and Information please contact our EU
representative GPSR@taylorandfrancis.com
Taylor & Francis Verlag GmbH, Kaufingerstraße 24, 80331 München, Germany

www.ingramcontent.com/pod-product-compliance
Ingram Content Group UK Ltd.
Pitfield, Milton Keynes, MK11 3LW, UK
UKHW020934180425
457613UK00019B/399